RETROVERSION AND TEXT CRITICISM

SOCIETY OF BIBLICAL LITERATURE
SEPTUAGINT AND COGNATE STUDIES SERIES

Edited by
Claude Cox

Number 17

RETROVERSION AND TEXT CRITICISM

The Predictability of Syntax in an Ancient Translation from Greek to Ethiopic

by

John Russiano Miles

RETROVERSION AND TEXT CRITICISM

The Predictability of Syntax in an Ancient Translation from Greek to Ethiopic

by
John Russiano Miles

Scholars Press
Chico, California

Retroversion and Text Criticism

The Predictability of Syntax in an Ancient Translation from Greek to Ethiopic

by
John Russiano Miles

© 1985
Society of Biblical Literature

Library of Congress Cataloging in Publication Data

Miles, John Russiano
Retroversion and text criticism.

(Septuagint and cognate studies series ; 17)
Bibliography: p.
1. Bible. O.T. Esther—Translating. 2. Bible. O.T. Esther—Criticism, Textual. 3. Greek language—Translating into Ethiopic. 4. Ethiopic language—Translating. 5. Greek language—Syntax. 6. Ethiopic language—Syntax. I. Title. II. Series.
BS1375.2.M55 1985 222'.9046 85-8178
ISBN 0-89130-878-4 (alk. paper)
ISBN 0-89130-879-2 (pbk.)

Printed in the United States of America
on acid-free paper

for my mother

CONTENTS

Preface	ix
Transliteration Key	x
INTRODUCTION	1
CHAPTER ONE An Analysis of Greek-Ethiopic Translation Syntax in Esther 1-8	9
CHAPTER TWO Translation Decision Charts Derived from the Analysis of Greek-Ethiopic Translation Syntax in Esther 1-8	85
CHAPTER THREE A Prediction of the Ethiopic Syntax of Esther 9 from the Greek Text	125
CHAPTER FOUR A Prediction of the Greek Syntax of Esther 10 from the Ethiopic Text	157
CHAPTER FIVE A Prediction of the Ethiopic Syntax of III 'ezra 3 from the Greek Text and a Prediction of the Greek Syntax of IV Baruch 1 from the Ethiopic Text	177
NOTES	201
BIBLIOGRAPHY	211

Preface

The work before you is the slightly revised version of a doctoral dissertation accepted at Harvard in 1971. As the work is published, it is a pleasure to acknowledge a debt of gratitude to Professor Emeritus Thomas O. Lambdin, under whose direction I wrote it; to the editors of the series Septuagint and Cognate Studies, who encouraged its publication; and to those scholars and students who, as I hope, may read it.

In the decade since the work was written, the computer has become a more common tool of scholarship, and a new generation of students, better equipped to program my question than I was, may well find this study a bit simple-minded. I ask their indulgence and look forward, respectfully, to reading their work.

There are times when all questions seem to me to collapse into the question of translation and when to study even the most arcane aspect of translation is to cut to the quick of the human mind. When the answers offered in this study are laid aside, I hope that the question which prompted it may remain and that those who take it up may find in it as much fascination as I did twelve years ago.

J.R.M.

Malibu, California

March, 1983

TRANSLITERATION KEY

Ethiopic

ha hu hi hā hē h(e) ho . . . . ሀ ሁ ሂ ሃ ሄ ህ ሆ
la, etc. . . . . ለ etc.
ḥa, etc. . . . . ሐ etc.
ma, etc. . . . . መ etc.
śa, etc. . . . . ሠ etc.
ra, etc. . . . . ረ etc.
sa, etc. . . . . ሰ etc.
qa, etc. . . . . ቀ etc.
ba, etc. . . . . በ etc.
ta, etc. . . . . ተ etc.
xa, etc. . . . . ኀ etc.
na, etc. . . . . ነ etc.
'a, (but a in initial position). . . አ etc.
ka, etc. . . . . ከ etc.
wa, etc. . . . . ወ etc.
ʿa, etc. . . . . ዐ etc.
za, etc. . . . . ዘ etc.
ya, etc. . . . . የ etc.
da, etc. . . . . ደ etc.
ga, etc. . . . . ገ etc.
ṭa, etc. . . . . ጠ etc.
p̣a, etc. . . . . ጰ etc.
ṣa, etc. . . . . ጸ etc.
ḍa, etc. . . . . ፀ etc.
fa, etc. . . . . ፈ etc.
qwa, qwi, quā, qwē, qwe . . . . . . ቈ etc.
xwa, etc. . . . . ኈ etc.
kwa, etc. . . . . ኰ etc.
gwa, etc. . . . . ጐ etc.

<u>Greek</u>

a	α	m	μ
b	β	n	ν
g	γ	ks	ξ
d	δ	o	ο
e	ε	p	π
z	ζ	r	ρ
ē	η	s	σ, ς
th	θ	t	τ
i	ι	ph	φ
k	κ	kh	χ
l	λ	pa	ψ
u	υ	ō	ω
		ı	iota subscript

INTRODUCTION

"Mechanical translation" usually implies "inaccurate translation." However, the word "mechanical" of itself does not say anything worse than unoriginality; its opposite is not "accurate" but "playful" or "gratuitous." Within limits of fidelity to the sense of an original, a translation can be more or less mechanical, more or less creative. A poet will not translate like a translating machine. However, if the poet is skilled and if the machine works, the two will not differ from each other on a scale of accuracy but only on a scale of beauty. Both are within the range of fidelity to the prose meaning of the text. The poet must guard against putting more nuance into his translation than was in the original. The machine programmer must ask whether a too plain rendition of a beautiful text does not change even its plainest meaning. But these are cases which define the limits by breaking them.

What "mechanical" does imply is the composition of elements in a predetermined way. The transliteration keys on pp. x - xi makes the representation of Greek and Ethiopic words in Latin letters mechanical in this sense. It predetermines which Latin letters or combinations of letters will represent which Ethiopic and Greek letters; and once the table is drawn up, the representation does not change. Secondarily, then, "mechanical" says "predictable." Not everything which is predictable is mechanical because not everything which is predetermined is also composite. However, everything which is mechanical is also predictable.

If syntax is the composition of the elements of a language in at least a partially predetermined way, then in principle it should be possible to mechanize the translation of syntax. That is, it should be possible to plot the relationship between two syntaxes in a "syntacticon" which would function like a lexicon whose entries would be constructions instead of letters or words. By reference to this "syntacticon," the constructions necessary for a translation would be automatically available;[1] and secondarily, from any statement so translated, the syntax of the original would be recoverable.

A good "syntacticon," like a good lexicon, would have to be the *a posteriori* description of what translators do. However, it would not be unreasonable to begin by describing the syntactic habits of a translator who brought the constructions of his translation into something approaching a one-to-one correspondence with the constructions of his original.

Paradoxically, the translations which most nearly approximate this ideal are ancient translations of the Bible. The reason for this is that the Bible, while not unartistically composed, was not translated for the sake of its art. It was not the beauty of their work or its aesthetic effect on a reader or hearer that was foremost in the mind of the Bible readers and hearers but rather the content of the work and its moral effect. Translations of the Bible were made first for diaspora Jewish communities and later for converts to Christianity, for groups in other words who were interested in the content of the Bible, the "moral" of its stories, not in its excellence as *belles lettres*. The ancient translators were satisfied with their work at a point where a modern translator would begin to manipulate his, not to change the meaning but to create the proper aesthetic effect.

We may illustrate the difference with an ancient and a modern example: the Septuagint Greek translation of the Hebrew Psalm 137:1 and the first stanza of Rimbaud's "Le Bateau ivre" as translated by Louise Varèse.[2] First the Hebrew psalm:

ʻal naharôt bābel	*Epi tōn potamōn Babulōnos*
šām yāšabnu	*ekei ekathisamen*
gam bākînu	*kai eklausamen*
b^{e}zokrēnu ʼet ṣiyyôn.	*en tōͅ mēsthēnai hēmas tēs Sion*.

Here the translation parallels the structure of the original and is faithful to its meaning, but the aesthetic effect of the original is destroyed: the necessary insertion of three definite articles lengthens the Greek. The fact that the subject of the Greek infinitive is the pronoun hēmas rather than a form that would match the -amen -amen of the verbs means that the -nu-nu-nu parallelism of the Hebrew is lost. And, of course, the meter is gone. This destruction of the Hebrew aesthetic effect could have been remedied had the Greek been reworked with effect in mind. But this was not done. Nothing was done in the Greek but what was necessary to reproduce the prose meaning of the Hebrew poem.

The French poem:

Comme je descendais des Fleuves impassibles
As I came down the impassible Rivers

Je ne me sentis plus guidé par les haleurs
I felt no more the bargemen's guiding hands,

Des peaux-rouges criards les avaient pris pour cibles,
Targets for yelling redskins they were nailed

Les ayant cloués nus aux poteaux de couleurs.
Naked to painted poles.

Varèse's English does not parallel the French structure, though this would have been possible without loss of meaning; one may question whether the exact prose meaning has been preserved; but it is evident that in her translation a great effort has been made to duplicate the emotional and aesthetic effect of the original. The original "les haleurs" has become "the bargemen's guiding hands." The punctuation has been changed. The second sentence in the stanza has been shifted from active to passive. An attempt has been made to maintain a rhythm in English. One may question whether these and the other modifications of the translation have their intended effect. But it would be difficult to deny that modifications have been made beyond what would have been necessary to reproduce the prose meaning of the poem. Translated as the psalm is translated, the poem would read:

As I came down the impassible Rivers,
I did not feel myself any longer guided by the bargemen:
Yelling redskins had taken them for targets,
Having nailed them naked to painted poles.

If these two translations of Rimbaud had been written by the same person, the second translation would undoubtedly have been written first, for nothing that is achieved in it is not achieved in the the first translation, while much is achieved in the first that is not attempted in the second. Practical experience in translation suggests that the first draft is always formally the closest to the original while subsequent drafts vary the form to make the meaning more exact and the aesthetic effect more appropriate. The point to be made is that ancient translations are not doing something different from modern translations: they are doing the same thing but cutting the process off sooner. If one could reduce the syntactic habits of an ancient translator to mechanical steps, he could be giving at the same time a description of the first step in a modern translator's activity.

In the study which follows, we attempt to give a description of how the syntax of the Book of Esther was translated from Greek into Ethiopic. The history of the translation of the Bible into Ethiopic is problematic, and not every scholar regards Greek as the language -- or the only language -- from which the translation was made.[3] However, the original language of at least the Book of Esther almost undoubtedly was Greek. Not only does the Ethiopic version include the so-called Greek additions (material found in the Septuagint version but not in the Hebrew), it also gives proper names in the Greek form: Mordecai is *mardokēyos* or *mardokēwos* from the Greek *Mardokhaios*, and less familiar names often appear with a Greek case ending; e.g. (A:1) *Mardokhaios ho tou Iairou* does not become *mardokēwos za'iya'iros* but *mardokēwos za'iya'iru*. The editor of the Ethiopic translation writes:

> La...version éthiopienne suit de très près le texte grec des LXX; l'interprète a traduit très littéralement le texte, de manière qu'il est presque toujours possible de deviner les mots grecs que l'interprète avait sous les yeux.[4]

How and to what extent a modern critic can hope to discern

the words which an ancient translator had *sous les yeux* as he began his work is precisely the question to which our analysis of syntax is finally addressed. Accordingly, we have chosen a translation in which there is a high *prima facie* likelihood that such a discernment could take place. However, it is important to note at the outset that the task in hand is not the establishment of a textual witness to the LXX through "retroversion" from the Ethiopic.

Our concern is rather with "retroversion" as a more general problem in critical method. Briefly, we submit that if the modern critic can get from translation to original, it can only be because he knows how a given ancient translator got from original to translation; and that since this knowledge can only be acquired when both the original and the translation are available for study. his ability to "retrovert" results less from insight into the translation he is considering, presumably one for which the original is lost, than it results from insight transferred from his work on other translations for which the originals were available.

The bulk of the thesis is an attempt at a small working model of how this transferral might take place. In place of a corpus of translations with extant originals, we take Esther 1-9. In place of a translation of the same type but without extant original, we take Esther 10. In our first two chapters, we attempt to spell out as exactly as possible just how the syntax of the original becomes the syntax of the translation. In our third chapter, we test our findings by attempting to predict the Ethiopic syntax of Esther 9 from the Greek. In our fourth chapter, we apply our findings to the task of the "recovery" of the Greek syntax of Esther 10.

Our heuristic expectation throughout is that in a mechanical translation, the translator will always choose that construction in the translation language which is formally closest to the construction he faces in the original. When he does not do this, there is always a reason: *something would happen* in the translation if he did. Every circumlocution is a detour, in other words.

De facto, not every circumlocution is a detour, and our heuristic expectation is that we will not always find what we are looking for. For the ancient translators did not consciously strive for the mechanical. They simply did not consciously avoid it. They were spontaneously mechanical, so to speak, without being obliged to avoid every gratuitous circumlocution.

It goes without saying that the Goettingen edition of Septuagint Esther which we use in constructing our model is not exactly the text which the Ethiopian translator of the Book of Esther had before his eyes. Similarly, it goes without saying that Pereira's Ethiopic text is not in exactly the form in which the ancient translator left it. However, in a methodological exercise of the sort described, we are justified in treating them as if they were. The extent to which the two documents are or are not in their pristine state makes no difference to the task we are about so long as their present relationship can in some way be charted and so long as it can be reconstructed when, for the sake of the model, we regard one of the related members as lost.

It would be possible, of course, by deliberately choosing a "free" translation, to prejudice the outcome of our test *against* the viability of retroversion as a technique in text criticism. By the same token, in choosing a pair of texts whose syntactic and semantic relationship seemed transparent to the scholar who edited one of them for publication (and would seem so to most scholars), we might seem to prejudice the outcome of the test *in favor of* the viability of retroversion as a technique. In fact, we intend to prejudice the outcome in neither direction but only to begin with a simpler rather than a more complicated exercise.

If there is a second reason for our choice of texts, it might rest on the observation that even scholars who do practice retroversion and who do trust their intuition in this regard will admit that certain texts beggar intuition. It is not our intention to create some improved, more scientific form of retroversion so as to extend the technique to texts that now seem beyond its reach. We intend only, and simply, to create a model of the kind of retroversion that scholars actually attempt. The pairing of the Greek and the Ethiopic Esther is, so to speak, within that range.

Indirectly, our analysis of syntactic relationships between the Greek and the Ethiopic forms of the Book of Esther serves a second scholarly purpose. Ethiopic literature is unusual in having begun with translations from the Greek, and it is not unreasonable to expect the grammar of at least the written form of the language to show signs of Greek influence. To date, however, none of the grammars of Ethiopic has taken systematic account of this possibility. To do so, the grammarian would have to compare Ethiopic translations from the Greek with their Greek originals and with original Ethiopic compositions. Much of the discussion in our first chapter relates at least as much to the first step in this process of comparison as it does to the problem of "retroversion" in text criticism.

CHAPTER ONE

An Analysis of Greek-Ethiopic Translation Syntax in Esther 1-8

For purposes of translation analysis, Greek syntax in Esther 1-8 will be considered under the following headings:

I.	Verb-to-verb subordination	11
	A. Verb + participle	11
	B. Verb + infinitive	15
	C. Verb + conjunction + finite verb	20
II.	Verb-to-substantive subordination	25
	A. Substantive + participle	25
	B. Substantive ± _hōste_ + infinitive	27
	C. Substantive + relative + finite verb	28
III.	Substantive-to-substantive subordination	30
	A. Substantive + genitive substantive	30
	B. Substantive + dative substantive	35
	C. Substantive + preposition + substantive	36
IV.	Substantive-to-verb subordination	38
	A. Active verb + dative object + direct object	41
	B. Active verb + dative object used alone	49
	C. Passive verb + dative object	52
	D. Verb + adverbial dative	54
	E. Verb + accusative used alone	54
	F. Verb + preposition + substantive	57
	G. Verb + genitive substantive	59
V.	Adjective-to-substantive subordination	61
VI.	Substantive-to-adjective subordination	67
	A. Substantive + adjective + complement	67
	B. Substantive + adjective + preposition	67
VII.	Coordination of sentences	68

VIII. Formulaic language 69

A. Date formulae 69

B. Time formulae 74

C. Formulae connected with kingship 75

D. Weight formulae 76

E. Genealogical formulae 76

F. Formulae in reported speech 77

G. Epistolary conventions 78

H. Miscellaneous other formulae 78

IX. Omission, mistranslation, paraphrase, and unpredictable translation 81

I. VERB-TO-VERB SUBORDINATION.

A. Greek verb + participle[1]

1. Greek aorist predicative participle X + finite verb or infinitive Y. In the first eight chapters of LXX Esther, twenty-four occurrences of this construction are translated as follows:

(a) fourteen finite verb X + finite verb Y

(b) four finite verb Y + soba + finite verb X

(c) five gerund X + finite verb Y

(d) one finite verb X + enza + imperfect Y.

(a,c) The two basic translation constructions are (a) and (c), reflecting an Ethiopic semantic distinction within the area of meaning covered by the Greek aorist participle. When the action of the aorist participle is simply ended before the action of the finite verb or infinitive begins, the Ethiopic translates by verb X + verb Y; e.g. (A:14),

homologēsantes apēkhthēsan.	wa'amnu watakwannanu.
"Having confessed, they were led off (to prison)."	"And they confessed and were condemned."

When the action of the participle though completed has effects that continue during the action of the main verb, the Ethiopic translates by gerund X + verb Y; e.g. (B:2),

pasēs epikratēsas oikoumenēs ebouleuthēn....	kwello baḥāwerta agrireya faqadku....
"Having mastered the whole world, I wished....	"Having mastered all lands, I wished....

(b). The occurrences of (b), e.g. (4:4),

etarakhthē akousasa to gegonos,	dangaḍat soba sam'at zanta zakama kona,

probably result from the translator's wish to avoid making the distinction we have just spoken of. soba, as the most general of the temporal conjunctions, could be the equivalent of either (a) or (c).

(*d*). In the remaining instance (4:1),

kai ekpēdēsas	*waroṣa*
dia tēs plageias tēs poleōs	*enta marxeba hagar*
eboa phōnē̜ megalē̜,	*enza yeṣarex ba'abiy qāl*,
"And having run through	"And he ran
the square of the city,	through the square of the city
he cried with a loud voice,"	while crying with a loud voice,"

the Greek participle is used loosely, and neither of the available Ethiopic translations would have been comprehensible; i.e., both would have put the subject outside the town square when he shouted. A translation on the model of the present participle is substituted.

2. Greek verb X + present predicative participle Y. In the first eight chapters of LXX Esther, twenty-three occurrences of this construction are translated into Ethiopic as follows:
   - (a) eight verb X + *enza* + imperfect Y
   - (b) two imperfect X + imperfect Y
   - (c) one verb X + *zabo*
   - (d) one verb X + *esma* + imperfect Y
   - (e) one verb X + *kama* + subjunctive Y
   - (f) four verb X + *kama* + imperfect Y
   - (g) five finite verb XY
   - (h) one *kona* + adjective Y.

(*a,b*). In seven of the eight occurrences of (a), Greek X is an aorist finite verb or infinitive; e.g. (C:1),

kai edeēthē kuriou	*wasa'ala*
mnēmoneuōn panta ta erga kuriou.	*enza yezēker kwello zakama gabra egzi'abḥēr*.
"And he prayed the Lord	"And he prayed
remembering all the works	while remembering how much
of the Lord."	God had done."

In one of the two occurrences of (b), Greek X is a present

finite verb; in the other it is an imperfect; e.g. (D:4),

hē de hetera epēkolouthei kouphizousa tēn endusin autēs.	*wakāle'tā tetlewā wateṣawer albāsihā.*
"And the other was following, supporting her garment."	"And her other one was following her and supporting her garments."

The distinction being made is probably aspectual. In (a), where X has a punctual aspect, Y a durative aspect, the two are translated by Ethiopic perfect X + imperfect Y and separated (or joined) by *enza*. In (b), where Greek X and Y both have a durative aspect, both are translated by the Ethiopic imperfect in simple parallel.

The remaining occurrence of (a), (6:9),

kai kērussetō dia tēs plateias legōn,	*wayesbek lotu'awādi westa marḥeba hagar enza yebel*,
"And let him herald (him) through the square saying..,"	"And let a herald announce him in the square of the city while saying..,"

does not really violate the rule; for the Ethiopic subjunctive, as a development from the older preterite/jussive *yaqtul*, retains a punctual aspect.

(*c*). In (c), Y is Greek *ekhōn*; scil.. (8:15),

ho de Mardokhaios eksēlthen... stephanon ekhōn khrusoun.	*wawaḍ'a mardokēwos... zabo aklila warq.*
"And Mordecai went out having a golden crown."	"And Mordecai went out having a golden crown."

(*d,e*). The Ethiopic construction *enza* + verb is always a temporal clause of contemporaneity or a mild adversative, like English *while*. The Greek present participle, on the other hand, covers other semantic areas including, as in the present sample, purpose and cause. In these areas, Ethiopic has to specify -- as in (c) and (d) -- by *esma*, *kama*, etc., and the appropriate form of the finite verb.

(f). The four occurrences of (f) translate Greek verb of statement X + accusative substantive + accusative present predicative participle, e.g. (3:4),

hupedeiksan tọ Aman	nagarewwo lahāmā
Mardokhaion tois tou basileōs	kama ya'abi mardokēwos
logois antitassomenon.	te'ezzāza neguś.
"And they indicated to Haman	"And they told Haman
that Mordecai resisted the	that Mordecai resisted
orders of the king."	the order of the king."

(g). Of the five occurrences of (g), one translates Greek X + cognate participle Y; scil., (6:13),

enōpion autou pesōn pesẹ̄	qedmēhu wadaqqa
"Falling you will fall	"You will fall before him."
before him"	

The remaining four translate the Greek periphrastics; e.g. (4:2),

ou gar ēn ekson autọ̄	esma iyekaweno labawi'.
eiselthein.	
"For it was not possible for	"Because it was not possible for
him to go."	him to go."

Where X is Greek einai, the translation cannot use enza: ihallawa enza...would mean "he was not in existence while he...."

(h). (h) is also a periphrastic using (understood) einai but one in which Y is a present passive participle. Translation is by kona + adjective rather than by the t-form apparently to preserve the quasi-stative quality of the passive participle; scil., (D:5),

hē de kardia autēs	walebbā-sa
apestenōmenē apo tou phobou.	ḥezun emferhat.
("Her face was happy.)	("Her face was joyful,)
but her heart was contracted	but her heart was saddened
with fear."	with fear."

B. Greek verb + infinitive.

1. Greek verb of intent X ± dative object ± hōste + aorist or present infinitive Y. In the first eight chapters of LXX Esther, sixty-three occurrences of this construction are translated into Ethiopic by verb X ± kama + subjunctive Y.

Formally, the translation construction closest to the Greek is Ethiopic verb X + infinitive Y. Semantically, however, the infinitive is not felt to be a subjunctive without specification to person and tense but rather a similarly unspecified indicative. And therefore it is not an adequate translation for those occurrences of the Greek infinitive which, since they follow verbs of intention, have only an intentional reality.

The difference between the subjunctive and the infinitive appears in the following pair of translations (A:6 and A:8):

hētoimasthē pan ethnos eis polemon hōste polemēsai dikaion ethnos	taḍalawu ḥezb laṣabe' kama yeṣbe'ewwomu laḥezb ṣadqān
"Every nation was prepared for war, to make war on a just people";	"The nations were prepared for war to make war on a just people";
hētoimasthēsan apolesthai kai eboēsan pros ton theon	taḍalawu lataḥagwelo waṣarxu xaba egzi'abḥēr
"They were ready to die, and they cried out to God."	"They were ready to die and they cried out to God."

In the first occurrence, hetoimasthenai expresses intent on the part of the warring peoples. In the second occurrence, it does not express intent: the people obviously do not want to die and are calling on God to save them. hetoimasthenai in this second instance is used modally: "The people were about to die, in danger of destruction," etc.

There are three basic forms of the translation construction verb X ± kama + subjunctive Y. When the subject of X and Y is the same, Y agrees in person and number with X; e.g. (3:6),

ebouleusato	fagada
aphanisai pantas tous Ioudaious.	yāṭfe'omu lakwellomu ayhud.
"He wanted to destroy all the Jews	"He desired that he should destroy all the Jews.

When the subject of Y is different from that of X and is expressed in a dative object of X, Y agrees with the dative object; e.g. (A:16),

epetaksen ho basileus Mardokhaiǭ	azzazo neguš lamardokēwos
therapeuein.	yeṣṣamad.
"The king ordered Mordecai to serve."	"The king ordered Mordecai that he should serve."

When the subject of Y is different from that of X but not expressed, Y is in the third person plural; e.g. (3:9),

dogmatisatō	ya'azzez
apolesai autous.	yāṭfe'ewwomu.
"Let him give the command to kill them."	"Let him command that they should kill them."

The last form of the translation construction is an impersonal usage. However, it would appear that in Ethiopic the usage is understood to stand for some actual but undefined third-person group. This at any rate would explain the translation (4:4),

apesteilen	fannawat albāsa lamardokēwos
stolisai ton Mardokhaion.	zayelabes.
"She sent to have Mordecai clothed."	"She sent clothes for Mordecai to put on."

Here the third plural usage, though possible, is avoided, because though Esther is sending garments to the ragged Mordecai, no third-person group will actually dress him. The standard translation is changed to avoid suggesting this.

The nuance of meaning separating Greek verb of intent +

infinitive from Greek verb of intent + hōste + infinitive is not reflected in the Ethiopic, which translates both by the subjunctive. The difference between the aorist and the present infinitive is also lost since there is only one tense of the Ethiopic subjunctive. kama is optional in the translation since the meaning can be carried by the subjunctive alone.

2. Greek verb of conation or possibility X + infinitive Y. Six occurrences of this construction in the first eight chapters of Esther are translated by:
   (a) five verb X ± la + infinitive Y.
   (b) one verb X + ba-infinitive Y.

(a). Group (a) includes the use of hetoimasthenai referred to above as modal. By a modal usage, we understand a verbal hendiadys in which the formally dependent member is semantically the more important. Thus in the English sentence, "I can speak," "speak" is the modified element. The sentence puts a modality on the action of speaking, not on that of being able.

Different languages reduce different actions to modes, and an original semantic difference can become a formal habit as in the negligible difference between "I can speak" and "I am able to speak."

In Ethiopic, we would suggest that where the translator renders the Greek infinitive by an infinitive, he understands the Greek main verb to be modal; or at least, that the formal marker of modality in Ethiopic, the marker corresponding to the absence of "to" before the English infinitive, is the use of the infinitive.

In three occurrences of dunasthai, the modal use is indisputable; e.g. (6:13),

ou mē dunē̦ auton amunasthai.	itekel mawi'oto.
"You cannot defeat him."	"You cannot defeat him."

The modal translation of hetoimasthenai given above and our modal translation of speudein are more disputable; scil., (2;9),

espeusen autō dounai to smegma.	afṭana wehibotā gebe'a.
"He hastened to give her the ointment."	"He quickly gave her the ointment."

(b). The one occurrence of (b) is skopein (E:7):

skopein de eksestin.	baxalleyo baḥtu yekawen.
"It is possible to see."	"In thinking, however, it is possible."

The construction ba-infinitive may be regarded as the form the modal phrase takes when the modal verb itself is impersonal.

3. Greek verb of statement X + infinitive Y. A single occurrence in the first four chapters of Esther is translated by verb of statement X + kama + indicative Y; scil. (B:4),

epedeiksen hēmin... anamemikhthai dusmenē laon tina.	'ayd'ana kama...tadammara ḥezb za'ekuy hegu.
"He indicated to us that a harsh people was mingled (among the peoples of the world)."	"He told us that (among the peoples of the world) a people of evil habit was mixed."

Note that kama cannot be optional here and that the tense of the Greek infinitive can be reflected to some extent by varying the tense of the Ethiopic indicative.

4. Greek verb of action X + accusative + infinitive Y. Two occurrences of this construction in the first eight chapters of Esther are translated into Ethiopic by causative verb XY.

As statement is to intent, so causation is to conation or possibility. Ethiopic, however, does not express caused action by a syntactic construction but a distinct causal verb system from within its morphology; scil. (5:12),

epoiēsen auten prōteuein kai hēgeisthai tēs basileias.	a'bayo bawesta mangeštu.
"He made him be first and be a leader of the kingdom."	"He made him great in his kingdom."

5. Greek impersonal verb X + infinitive Y. A single occurrence of this construction in the first four chapters of LXX Esther is translated into Ethiopic by imperfect Y; scil. (1:15),

hōs dei poiēsai Astin tē basilissē.	zakama yerēseyewwā la'astin negešt.
"How it was neccessary to treat Vashti the queen."	"How they would treat Vashti the queen."

6. Greek verb X + preposition + infinitive Y. Nine occurrences of this construction in the first eight chapters of Esther are translated into Ethiopic as follows:
   (a) six verb X + conjunction + perfect Y
   (b) three verb X + conjunction + imperfect Y.

(a). (a) translates Greek aorist or perfect infinitive; e.g. (5:9),

en tō idein Aman Mardokhaion ...ethumōthē.	soba re'yo hāmā lamardokēwos ...tame''a.
"In Haman's seeing Mordecai ...he was angered."	"When Haman saw Mordecai, ...he was angered."

(b). (b) translates the Greek present infinitive; e.g. (6:4),

en de tō punthanesthai ton basilea	wa'enza'yetnāgar neguš
peri tēs eunoias Mardokhaiou	akwatēto lamardokēwos

ideu Aman en tē aulē. — basha hāmā westa 'aṣad.

"And as the king was being informed about Mordecai's goodwill, Haman appeared in court." — "And while the king was discussing the praise of Mordecai, Haman arrived in court."

C. Greek verb + conjunction + finite verb.

1. Greek verb X + object clause (conjunction + indicative Y, functioning together as direct object). Twenty-seven occurrences of this construction in the first eight chapters of LXX Esther are translated into Ethiopic as follows:
   (a) ten verb X + kama + indicative Y
   (b) ten verb X + zakama + indicative Y
   (c) four verb X + kwello za- + indicative Y
   (d) two verb X + kwello zakama + indicative Y
   (e) one verb X + yogi + indicative Y.

(a). The ten occurrences of (a) translate Greek indirect statements of fact using hoti; e.g. (3:5),

epignous Aman hoti ou proskunei autō Mardokhaios. — soba a'mara hāmā kama iyesaged lotu mardokēwos.

"Haman, having learned that Mordecai would not bow to him." — "When Haman learned that Mordecai would not bow to him."

The remaining twelve constructions translate indirect questions.

(b,c,e). Eight of nine occurrences of (b) translate indirect questions of manner or quality using hōs (four times), katha, hoia, and the cognate accusative;[2] e.g. (1:17),

diēgēsato autois ta hrēmata tēs basilissēs kai hōs anteipen tō basilei. — wanagaromu qāla lanegešt zakama abayato laneguš.

"He recounted to them the words of the queen — "And he told them the words of the queen

and how she contradicted the king."	how she contradicted the king."

The remaining occurrence of (b) and all the occurrences of (c) and (d) translate Greek indirect questions of quantity using hosa or its equivalent;[3] e.g. (4:17),

epoiēsen	gabra
hosa eneteilato autǭ Esthēr.	kwello za'azzazato Astēr.
"He did as much as Esther ordered him."	"He did everything that Esther ordered him."

(e). There remains one occurrence of Ethiopic verb X + yogi + indicative Y translating a Greek indirect question of fact; scil. (4:14)

tis oiden	mannu'a yā'amer'a
ei eis ton kairon touton	yogi'a bazentu'a mawā'el'a
ebasileusas	nagaški'a.
"Who knows whether up to this time you have reigned?"	"Who knows? Perhaps in these days you have reigned."

2. Greek verb X + adverbial clause (conjunction + finite verb Y functioning together as adverbial modifier). Thirty-eight occurrences of this construction in the first eight chapters of LXX Esther are translated into Ethiopic as follows:
   (a) four verb X + bakama + indicative Y
   (b) sixteen verb X + esma + indicative Y
   (c) four verb X + ema + indicative Y
   (d) two verb X + la'ema + indicative Y
   (e) four verb X + kama + subjunctive Y
   (f) five verb X + soba + indicative Y
   (g) one verb X + nāhu + indicative Y
   (h) one verb X + kama-sa + indicative Y
   (i) one verb X + enbala + indicative Y.

(a). The four occurrences of (a) translate adverbial

comparative clauses using *hōs*, *katha*, *kathōs*; e.g. (2:20),

eneteilato autȩ̄ Mardokhaios	*azzaza mardokēwos*
phobeisthai ton theon	*kama tefrah egzi'abḥēr*
kai poiein ta prostagmata autou	*wategbar te'ezzāzo*
kathōs ēn met autou.	*bakama hallawat meslēhu.*
"Mordecai ordered her	"Mordecai ordered her
to fear God	that she fear God
and keep his commandments	and keep his commandment
as (she had when) she was with him."	as (she had when) she was with him."

The difference between the object clause with *zakama* and the adverbial clause with *bakama* is the difference between English *how* and *as*. LXX Esther will often use the same word for both; e.g., *hōs* in 1:17 (cf. supra: C,1,b) and *hōs* in 3:12:

egrapsan	*ṣaḥafu*
hōs epetaksen Aman.	*bakama azzazomu hāmā*.
"They wrote	"They wrote
as Haman had ordered them."	as Haman had ordered them."

Ethiopic, however, like English, keeps the two notions explicitly distinct. 1:17 cannot be translated "He recounted to them the words of the queen *as* she had contradicted him" (*bakama*) but only "...*how* she had contradicted him" (*zakama*). 3:12 cannot be translated "They wrote *how* Haman had ordered them (*zakama*) but only "...*as* Haman had ordered them (*bakama*).

(*b*). The sixteen occurrences of (b) translate Greek causal clauses with *hoti* (thirteen), *dioti*, *anth hōn*, and *ei*; e.g. (C:8),

ho theos Abraam	*amlaka abrehām*
pheisai tou laou sou,	*maḥek ḥezbaka*
hoti epiblepousin hēmin	*esma qomu lāʿelēna*
eis kataphthoran.	*yāmāsenuna.*
"God of Abraham,	"Lord of Abraham,
spare your people	spare your people,
because they look upon us	because they rise against us.

for (our) destruction."	that they may destroy us."

(*c,d*). The four occurrences of (c) and the two of (d) translate Greek conditional clauses with *ean* + aorist subjunctive (two) and *ei* + present indicative (four); either Greek form may go with either Ethiopic form. One example (3:9):

ei dokei tǭ basilei	*wa'ema-sa fagada neguš*
dogmatisatō apolesai autous.	*ya'azzez wayāṭfe'omu.*
"If it seems right to the king	"And if the king wishes,
let him pass the decree to destroy them."	let him command that they kill them."

(*e*). The four occurrences of (e) translate Greek purpose clauses with *hina* + subjunctive; e.g. (C:7),

epoiēsa touto	*gabarkewwo lazentu*
hina mē thō doksan anthrōpou	*kama iyerassi kebra emmaḥeyāw*
huperanō doksēs theou.	*lā'ela emna kebra egzi'abḥēr.*
"I did this	"I did this
that I might not place the glory of man	that I might not place the glory of man
above the glory of God."	above the glory of God."

(*f*). The five occurrences of (f) translate Greek aorist indicative temporal clauses introduced by *hote* (two), *hōs* (two), and *hotan*; e.g. (5:13),

tauta moi ouk areskei	*iyehēwezani*
hotan idō Mardokhaion ton Ioudaion.	*soba re'ikewwo lamardokēwos ayhudāwi*.
"It does not please me	"It does not please me
when I see Mordecai the Jew."	when I see Mordecai the Jew."

(*g*). The one occurrence of (g) translates *ei* where the Greek conjunction does not introduce a condition but a fact given as the ground of an argument; scil. (8.7),

ei panta ta huparkhonta Aman edōka	*nāhu kwello newayo lahāmā*
kai ekharisamen soi...	*wahabkuki waṣagawkuki...*

ti eti eqizēteis?	*menta enka tefaqedi.*
"If I have given and granted you all the possession of Haman ...what more do you want?"	"Look, I have given and granted you all the property of Haman... What more do you want?"

(*h*). The one occurrence of (h) translates a general circumstantial clause introduced by *hōs*, "whereas." The sentence is lengthy and at some points the translation is inaccurate, but the use of *hōs* does seem accurately translated; (E:10),

hōs gar Aman... *etukhen*...*philanthropias*... *epetēdeusen tēs arkhēs sterēsai hēmas*....	*kama-sa hāmā*... *rakaba*...*šimata wameḥrata*... *xallaya yāwaḍe'ana emna mangeštena*....
"Whereas Aman... received...kindness... he plotted to deprive us of the realm...."	"Whereas Haman... received honor and kindness... he thought to expel us from our realm..."

(*i*). The one occurrence of (i) translates *enbala* + indicative; e.g. (C:29),

ouk ēuphranthē... *plēn epi soi, kurie*.	*itafaššeḥat* *enbala baka, egzi'o*.
"She did not rejoice... except in you, Lord."	"She did not rejoice except in you, God."

II. VERB-TO-SUBSTANTIVE SUBORDINATION.

A. Greek substantive + participle.

1. Greek substantive X + active participle Y. In the first eight chapters of Esther, twelve occurrences of this construction are translated into Ethiopic by: substantive X + za-finite verb Y; e.g. (A:12),

tōn duo eunoukhōn tou basileōs tōn phulassontōn tēn aulēn.	2 xeṣwanihu laneguš ella ya'aqehu hagara.
"The king's two eunuchs who were guarding the court."	"The king's two eunuchs who were guarding the city."

2. Greek substantive X + passive participle Y. In the first eight chapters of Esther, fourteen occurrences of this construction are translated into Ethiopic as follows:

(a) six substantive X + adjective

(b) four substantive X + za-passive finite verb Y

(c) four substantive X + za-active finite verb Y.

(a). Of the six occurrences of (a), five translate perfect passive participles; e.g. (3:8),

huparkhei ethnos diesparmenon.	hallo ḥezb 'alāwi.
"There exists a scattered people."	"There exists a rebellious people."

The remaining occurrence is a stative (E:16):

huious tou megistou hupsistou zōntos theou.	weluda egzi'abḥēr le'ul wa'abiy waḥeyāw.
"The sons of the great high living God."	"The sons of God the high and great and alive."

(*b*). In three of the four occurrences of (b), Y comes from roots in which the verbal adjective *qetul* -- the more frequent adjectival form in (a) -- has lost its participial character altogether to become simply an adjective and indeed frequently a nominalized adjective. The three roots are *l ' k*, *š y m*, and *f q r*; their *qetul* forms commonly mean, respectively, *legate* or *apostle*, *prefect*, and *friend*. The syntactic consequence of this lexical development is that the Ethiopic *qetul* form from these roots can no longer be modified as a verb. When the Greek participle is so modified, a relative clause must be substituted in the Ethiopic; e.g. (B:12),

tēn pothoumenēn *tois pasin anthrōpois* *eirēnēn*.	*salāma za'emxaba kwellu sabe'* *yetfāqar*.
"That peace which is desired by all men."	"That peace which is desired by all men."

In the remaining instance, (1:5),

tois ethnesin *tois heuretheisin* *eis tēn polin*,	*ḫezb* *ella tarakabu* *westa hagar*,
"the peoples found in the city,"	"the people found in the city,"

the Ethiopic *qetul* remains genuinely verbal, but it is also genuinely passive in a case where the Greek participle to be translated has a resultative-middle meaning. The Ethiopic form carrying this nuance of voice is the *t*-form, whence the translation.

(*c*). In one of the four occurrences of (c), (4:8),

kai to antigraphon *to en Sousois ektethen* *huper tou apolesthai autous*,	*maṣḥaf* *za'anbaru westa susā* *kama yeqtelewwemu*,
"the circular posted in Susa concerning their being destroyed,"	"the letter which they posted in Susa that they should kill them,"

the shift from the attested qetul form nebur to za- + finite verb is probably made necessary by the verbal modification; scil. because nebur is felt to be not a participle but simply an adjective. The further shift to the active impersonal then results from the fact that no t-form exists in a middle or passive sense from the root n b r, and the qal would be misleading.

In two further occurrences, E:17 and 8:5, the lexical question whether or not the qetul retains its participial character is cut short by a prior, more narrowly syntactic consideration. In these two occurrences, unlike any of the previous, the Greek participle is accompanied by an agent-phrase with hupo; and in Ethiopic -- as elsewhere in Semitic -- the expression of the agent of a passive verb is most uncommon.[5] To express the agent, Ethiopic has to put the sentences into the active voice; e.g. (8:5),

ta grammata ta apestalmena hupo Aman ta graphenta apolesthai tous Ioudaious.	maṣāḥefta zaṣaḥafa hāmā kama yeqtelewwomu la'ayhud.
"The letter which Haman dispatched that the Jews were to be destroyed."	"The letters which Haman wrote that they were to kill the Jews."

In the remaining occurrence, 6:2,

heuren de ta grammata ta graphenta peri Mardokhaiou,	wa'emze rakabu zawesta maṣāḥeft xaba ṣaḥafu ba'enta mardokēwos,
"he found the letter written concerning Mordecai.	"And then they found what was in the letters where they wrote concerning Mordecai,"

the circumlocution is most likely triggered by some less apparent lexical limitation of ṣeḥuf or taṣḥafa.

B. Greek substantive X ± hōste + infinitive Y. Four occurrences of this construction in the first eight chapters of Esther are translated by: substantive X ± kama + subjunctive Y; e.g. (8:5, E:11)

ta grammata	maṣāḥefta
ta apestalmena hupo Aman	zaṣaḥafa hāmā
ta graphenta	kama yeqtelewwomu
apolesthai tous Ioudaious;	la'ayhud;
"Letters	"The letters
written by Haman	that Haman wrote
to have the Jews killed";	that they should kill the Jews";
etukhen...philanthrōpias	šimata rakaba
epi tosouton	eska
hōste agoreuesthai hēmōn patera.	abuna nebēlo.
"he received...kindness	"he received honor
to the point	to the point that
of being called 'Our Father.'"	we said to him 'Our Father.'"

C. Substantive + relative + finite verb.

1. Substantive X + hos + ean + verb Y. In the first eight chapters of Esther, twenty-eight occurrences of this construction are translated into Ethiopic as follows:
   - (a) twenty-seven substantive X + za-finite verb Y
   - (b) one substantive X + emna-za-verb Y.

(b). The one occurrence of (b) is (6:10)

mē parapesatō sou logos	itexdeg aḥātta qāla
hōn elalēsas.	emna zanababka.
"Let there here not fall aside any word	"Do not omit a single word
which you have spoken."	from that which you have spoken."

The Greek relative is, of course, a genitive by attraction, an ellipsis for ...toutōn ha elalēsas. Presumably, the Ethiopic will always reflect this by the insertion of emna before the relative.

Examples of (a) (1:20, 6:7),

ho nomos ho hupo tou basileōs hon ean poiē en tē basileia autou;	zentu ḥeg zagabra neguš bamangeštu;
"The law of the king whatsoever he make in his kingdom";	"This law which the king made in his kingdom";
anthrōpon, hon ho basileus thelei doksasai.	labe'esi zayefaqed neguš yākbero.
"The man, whom the king wishes to honor."	"The man whom the king wishes that he might honor."

2. Greek substantive X + relative adverb + finite verb Y.

Four occurrences of this construction are all translated into Ethiopic by substantive X + conjunction + finite verb Y; e.g. (4,3)

en pasē khōra hou eksetitheto ta grammata.	bakwellu baḥāwert xaba tafannawa maṣāḥeft.
"In every place where these letters were published."	"In all lands where the letters were sent."

III. SUBSTANTIVE-TO-SUBSTANTIVE SUBORDINATION.

A. Greek substantive + genitive substantive.

1. Greek noun X + genitive substantive Y. Two-hundred-seventy-two occurrences of this construction in the first eight chapters of Esther are translated as follows:

(a) one-hundred-twenty-four X-suffix Y

(b) two substantive X + za-suffix Y

(c) ninety-three construct substantive X + substantive Y

(d) thirty-six substantive X-suffix + la-substantive Y

(e) seven substantive X + za-substantive Y

(f) two substantive X + em-substantive Y

(g) four kama + subjuntive X + subject/object Y

(h) four indicative verbal transformations.

(a,b). The occurrences of (a) all translate Greek X + personal prounoun Y, including autos and heautos. The occurrences of (b) also translate Greek X + autos in the genitive. The reason for the translation variance is probably the fact that in both the latter cases the Greek article has demonstrative force. X in one case in Greek definite noun repeating an indefinite noun; viz., (A:6),

kai egeneto autōn phōnē megalē	wakona qālomu 'abiya
kai tę phōnę autōn	wabaqāla zi'ahomu
hētoimasthē pan ethnos	tadalawu ḥezb
eis polemon.	laṣabe'.
"Then there was a great cry from them,	"Then there was a great cry from them
and with this great cry of theirs	and with this great cry of theirs
the whole nation was prepared for war."	the nation was prepared for war."

In the other case, X is a definite noun again repeating a less definite expression, this time a finite verb; viz. (1:8),

houtōs de ēthelēsen ho basileus	*alla bakama faqada we'etu neguš*
kai epetaksen tois oikonomois	*wa'azzazo lamagabtu*
poiēsai to thelēma autou.	*yegbaru faqago zi'ahu.*
"And thus the king wished, and he commanded his ministers	"But as the king wished, he commanded his ministers
to meet this wish of his."	to do this wish of his."

The shift in Greek from a phrase without the article (*autōn phōnē*) to one with it (*tȩ̄ phōnȩ̄ autōn*) gives the article a demonstrative force. Ethiopic, without a definite article, approximates this shift by a shift from substantive-suffix (*gālomu*) to substantive + *za*-suffix (*gāl zi'ahomu*).

(*c,d*). The occurrences of (c) constitute the construction which is formally closest to the Greek and may be regarded as its mechanical equivalent. In the occurrences of (d), Y is always a person. Though (c) is often used where Y is a person, e.g. (1:15),

tōn arkhontōn persōn kai mēdōn,	*lamakwānenta fārs wamēdon,*
"Of the rulers of the Persians and Medes,"	"Of the rulers of Persia and Media,"

(d) can *only* be used under this condition, e.g. (1:10),

tois hepta eunoukheis...	*la 7 xeswānihu*
tou basileōs.	*laneguš.*
"To the seven eunuchs	"To the 7 eunuchs
of the king."	of the king."

The difference in Ethiopic between X-*a* + Y, *bēta neguš*, and X-suffix + *la*-Y, *bētu laneguš*, is something like the difference between the English genitive X's + Y, "the king's house," and the prepositional idiom X *of* Y, "the house of the king." The Ethiopic expression with *la*-, like the English expression with *'s*, is primarily referred to personal possession. Qualification, specification, inclusion -- any genitive relationship other than that of active possession -- are expressed by X-a = Y, the equivalent of the English prepositional usage.

Obviously, one may speak of a person without speaking of active personal possession. Just as obviously, however, one cannot speak of active, personal possession without speaking of a person. Whence, as already noted, Y is always a person in (d), Y may be a person in (c).

The difference between (c) and (d) is a difference in point of view. "The palace of the king," "the king's palace," and "the royal palace" do not have the same meaning, though the same object is referred to in all three. What varies is the extent to which the speaker intends to direct his hearers' attention to the person of the king. The speaker's decision in this regard may not be important to him, but the structure of the language forces him to make it. In other words, in a given context, there may be little to choose between "the king's palace," "the palace of the king," and "the royal palace"; but the speaker must nonetheless choose.

Most often, however, where a language offers several choices, one choice will be more appropriate in a given situation. Were it not so, there would be no way in language to distinguish between, e.g., person and a personification like "the palace's king." Trying to discover a pattern of appropriateness in the first eight chapters of Esther, we find three occurrences of bēta neguš (A:3, 1:6, 3:4) and one each of mazgāba neguš (3:9), xoxta neguš (4:2), and ʿaṣada neguš as against none of bētu laneguš, mazgābu laneguš, etc. The latter expressions, though not impossible, are apparently felt to be less appropriate, possible because the noun that precedes neguš is in every case an institution that does not involve the person of the king but only, as it were, his royalty. They should be translated "the royal palace," "the royal treasury," "the royal gate," and "the royal court."[6,7]

At the other extreme, we may perhaps see manfaso laneguš as a phrase that would only much less appropriately be expressed by the construct; scil. (D:8),

kai metebalen ho theos to pneuma tou baileōs eis prautēta.	wamēṭa egzi'abḥēr manfaso laneguš westa yāwhāt.
"And God changed the king's spirit into mildness."	"And God changed the king's spirit into mildness."

In between are such patternings as three occurrences of daggu/dagigu laneguš, "the king's courtiers" (2:2, 6:3, 6:5), against one of dagga neguš, "the royal courtiers" (6:8), and four occurrences of xeṣwānihu laneguš, "the king's eunuchs" (A:12, 1:1, 1:10, 2:21) against two of xeṣwa neguš, "the royal eunuch" (2:3, 2:14).

(e). Six of seven occurrences of Ethiopic X + za-Y result simply from the circumstance that X is a proper name, and hence neither the construct with -a nor the construction with la- is available; e.g. (A:1),

enupnion eiden Mardokhaios ho tou Iairou tou Semeiou tou Kisaiou.	re'ya ḥelma mardokēwos za'iya'iru zasēmyo zaqēsyo.
"Mordecai the son of Iairos, the son of Semeios, the son of Kisaios, saw a dream."	"Mordecai the son of Iyairu, the son of Semyo, the son of Qēsyo, saw a dream."

In the remaining occurrence (8:2),

kai katestēsen Esthēr Mardokhaion epi pantōn tōn Aman,	wasēmato astēr lamardokēwos lā'ela kwellu zahāmā,
"Esther put Mordecai in charge of everything of Haman's,"	"Esther put Mordecai in charge of everything of Haman's,"

neither of the conventional translations of the Greek genitive is available. The construct is unavailable because the personal suffix has been permanently added to the noun kwel, making it impossible to add the -a of the construct. The construction with la- is unavailable since the permanent addition of the suffix has meant a reduction or at any rate a change in the force of the suffix to that of person- and number-marker on what is effectively an adjective. In other words, the suffix + la- in kwellu lahāmā does not have the sense it would have in bētu lahāmā. The translator's solution is to use the relative za-.

(f). The preposition emna is inserted between X and Y when X is the number aḥadu; e.g. (6:9),

kai dotō heni	wayahabewwo la 1
tōn philōn tou basileōs.	em'ā'rekta neguš.
"And let him give to one	"And let them give it to one
of the friends of the king."	of the friends of the king."

(g). Greek substantive X + genitive substantive Y after the prepositions eis and pros can express purpose. When it does, the Ethiopic translates by kama + subjunctive. If Y is a subjective genitive, it is translated as the subject of the subjunctive. If it is an objective genitive, it is translated as the object; e.g. a subjective genitive (C:6),

ēudokoun	abdarku
philein pelmata pedōn autou	es'am egārihu
pros sōtērian Israel.	kama yeḥyaw esra'ēl.
"I had been willing	"I had preferred
to kiss the soles of his feet	that I would kiss his feet
for the salvation of Israel."	that Israel might live."

(h). The three indicative verbal transformations are explained by the lack of Ethiopic nouns with the meaning required by the Greek. Consider 2:12:

houtōs gar anaplērountai	esma maṭanaze
hai hēmerai	mawā'el yenaberu
tēs therapeias.	enza yetḥērasā wayeššēnayā.
"For thus were completed	"Because up to that point
the days	lasted the days
of the treatment."	during which they were cultivated

and beautified."

ḥ r s may not be the only Ethiopic root available for the notion "care, treatment," therapeuein. However, if in the translator's mind, it was the correct one, he was in a bind; for no noun from that root exists in a meaning correspondeing to therapeia.

Similarly 7:2:

kai ti to aksiōma sou?	wamenta we'etu zatastabqwe'i,
"And what is your request?"	"And what is it that you request?"

b qw ' may, again, not be the only Ethiopic root available for the notion "request." However, if the translator thought it was, he was forced to a verbal translation; for no b qw ' noun exists in the meaning "a request," aksiōma.

2. Greek nominalized article X + genitive substantive Y. One occurrence of this construction in the first eight chapters of Esther is translated by substantive Y in the syntactic position indicated by Greek X; e.g. (2:22),

kai autē ephanison tǭ basilei ta tēs epiboulēs.	waye'eti ayde'ato laneguš mekromu.
"And she revealed to the king the nature of the plot."	"And she let the king know about their plot."

ta in the Greek is in the accusative, and so mekr is made the object of the Ethiopic sentence.

B. Greek substantive X + dative substantive Y. Fifteen occurrences of this construction in the first eight chapters of Esther are translated as follows:

(a) thirteen substantive + la + substantive Y

(b) one substantive X-suffix + la-substantive Y

(c) one substantive X-suffix.

(a) may be regarded as the standard translation; e.g. (8:16),

tois Ioudaiois	wala'ayhud-sa
egeneto phōs	kona berhān
"For the Jews	"And for the Jews,
there was light."	there was light."

(b) and (c) are both dative possessives and are translated as genitives; scil. (2:5, 3:10),

kai onoma autō Mardokhaios;	zasemu mardokēwos;
"His name was Mordecai";	"His name was Mordecai";
edōken eis kheira tō Aman.	wamaṭṭawo westa edēhu lahāmā
"He gave it into Haman's hand."	"He gave it into Haman's hand."

C. Greek substantive X + preposition + substantive Y. Forty-two occurrences of this construction in the first eight chapters of Esther are translated into Ethiopic as follows:

(a) thirty-seven substantive X + preposition + substantive Y

(b) two substantive-ni + wa-substantive-ni

(c) two substantive + za-substantive Y

(d) one substantive X + kama + subjunctive Y

(a). The first translation is the mechanical equivalent; e.g. (1:8),

ho de potos houtos	waba'ālu-sa
ou kata prokeimenon nomon.	ako haḅega qadāmi.
"And this banquet	"And this banquet
was not according to the previous manner."	was not according to the previous manner."

(b). The two occurrences of the post-positive particle -ni are in the single phrase (1:20):

tois andrasin heautōn	amtātihon
apo ptōkhou heōs plousiou.	bā'el-ni wanaddāy-ni.
"To their husbands	"Their husbands
from rich to poor."	both rich and poor."

A literal translation of the Greek would have used emna...wa'eska; but for the expression of a whole by its extremes, emna...wa'eska was not semantically available.[8]

(c). In one of the two translations by za-, namely (3:12),

tois arkhousin kata pasan khōran,	lamasāfent zakwellu beḥāwart,
"The rulers according to place,"	"The rulers of every place,"

the Ethiopic translator was faced with a dilemma stemming from the fact that lala-, the Ethiopic distributive corresponding mechanically to the Greek kata with the accusative, is always followed directly by a substantive. lalabaḥāwert would have been perfectly adequate to the Greek meaning but on the formal level would have left the translation without a word corresponding to the Greek pasan. Translating pasan by kwellu meant that the prepositional construction had to be abandoned, again a departure from the mechanical ideal, but one apparently felt to be smaller.

(d). In the one occurrence of (d), the infinitive is translated as indicated above (I,B); scil. (4:8),

kai to antigraphon to en Sousois ektethen huper tou apolesthai autous edōken autō deiksai tē Esthēr.	waqāla nagarā laye'eti maṣḥaf za'anbaru westa susā kama yeqtelewwomu wawahabo ar'ayāhā yār'eyā la'astēr.
"And the copy posted in Susa concerning their destruction he gave him to show Esther."	"And the words of the text of the letter that they posted in Susa (were) that they were to kill them. And he gave him a copy of it to show it to Esther."

IV. SUBSTANTIVE-TO-VERB SUBORDINATION.

Our analysis of verbal complements in Ethiopic Esther 1-8 takes three statements as starting point:

first, the analytic complement on the noun (substantive X-suffix + *la*-substantive Y) and the analytic complement on the verb (verb X-suffix + *la*-substantive Y) are too similar for them not to have, at least originally, a similar distribution;

second, the analytic noun complement distributes along an animation parameter, while the analytic verb complement does not;

third, most of the Greek datives in Esther 1-8 are translated by the analytic complement or some other construction involving the preposition *la*-.

The first statement is probably *a priori* (but see below, p. 47).

The first half of the second statement is proven by our own analysis (above III, A) and by evidence collected by H. Schneider in *L'Expression des compléments de verbe et de nom et la place de l'adjectif épithète en guèze*. Schneider attributes to the analytic complement on the noun and the verb alike "une valeur insistante" (p. 71). However, among one-hundred-eighty-six examples of the analytic complement on the noun, he finds one-hundred-seventy-one that refer to "living beings or groups of beings" (p. 50); and the figure is probably low, for of the five examples he gives from the fifteen occurrences referring "to a thing or an abstraction," four are taken from the Book of the Mysteries of Heaven and Earth, a work with a very poetic style. Schneider himself comments in his summation (p. 73),

> On ne trouve pas non plus de changements notables selon les différentes genres, sauf parfois, semble-t-il dans le Livre des Mystères, ouvrage apocalyptique rempli de visions, où des tournures plus expressives se rencontrent facilement.

It is easy enough to suppose that non-animate beings are spoken of as animate for poetic effect in examples such as (p. 50)[9];

faṭara ... 'amdā lanafs	"(God) created Wind's pillar";
wasemu lawe'etu 'eḍ	"And the name of the tree
zabal'u adām waḥēwān....	that Adam and Eve ate was...."

In Schneider's remaining example (p. 50),[10]

xwelqomu lawarq waberur	"La quantité de l'or et de l'argent
za'amṣe'u,	qu'ils apportèrent (et qu'on leur avait reclamé),"

his parenthetical qualification is at odds with his translation. Taking the parenthesis seriously, as indicating the context, we should rather translate,

"Their quota in gold and silver,
which they brought...."

Among the remaining ten occurrences, which are not listed, there may be some in which the complement is more clearly non-animate. But at worst, the distribution is 176/10, which with the 36/0 distribution from our own analysis establishes a fairly clear animation parameter for the use of the analytic complement after the substantive.

The second half of the second statement, namely, that the animation parameter is not observed by the analytic complement after the verb, is proven by occurrences such as the following from Esther C:3 and C:10:

ou polēso auta	*igabarkewwo lazentu ana*
en huperēphanią;	*bate'bit*
"I did not do it	"I did not do this
in pride."	in pride";
hilasthēti tō klērō sou	*tašāhal ḥezbaka*
kai strepson to penthos hēmōn	*wamiṭo lalāḥena*
eis euōkhian	*westa tefšeḥt*
hina zōntes	*kama baḥeywatena*
humnōmen sou to onoma;	*neṣabbeh lasemeka;*
"Be propitious to your people	"Be propitious to your people
and turn our mourning	and change our mourning
into joy	into joy

that living we may sing praise to your name";	that in our life we may praise your name";

and by occurrences such as the following from Schneider (pp.27 and 31)[11]:

wakwellu zayeṣawero waye'anego lazentu maṣḥaf yaḥayu;	"Everyone who will carry this book and suspend it from his neck will live";
kama yānberā laṣagwera bage' ḍamra ma'ekala zare'a garāht.	"(The sign will be) that he will place the pelt of a sheep, a fleece, in the middle of a planted field (lit. the growth of a field)."

In all these, the analytic complement is used where the complement is inanimate. The last example is particularly instructive, for it shows an analytic and a synthetic (accusative) complement in apposition.

The third of the statements constituting our starting point was that most of the Greek datives in Esther 1-8 are translated by the analytic complement or some other construction involving la-. Specifically, of seventy-seven datives in the Greek construction verb X + dative object Y + direct object Z, fifty-three are translated with la-. Of the remaining twenty-four, twenty-three are pronominal suffixes; only one Greek dative is translated by the Ethiopic accusative. Similarly, of sixty-nine datives in the Greek construction verb X + dative object Y, thirty-six are translated with la-, and of the remaining thirty-three datives, only four are translated by the Ethiopic accusative.

Our hypothesis is that the original value determining the use of the analytic complement after both the noun and the verb is animation. This value is blurred when an association grows up between the analytic complement after the verb and the Greek dative. As a result of this association, the analytic complement becomes available for the translation of the dative as such; i.e., whether or not the dative refers to an animate being. Finally, once the analytic complement has actually been used to translate a Greek dative with an inanimate referent, the way is cleared for a re-interpretation of usage in which the analytic and the synthetic complements are equally available in all situations.

The linchpin of the hypothesis, obviously, is the association of the Greek dative with the Ethiopic la-forms and especially with the analytic complement itself. We have noted the statistical predominance of this association. The association may be shown in another way, however; and to show it, we turn to the constructions themselves.

A. Greek active verb X + dative object Y + direct object Z (accusative or clause). Seventy-seven occurrences of this construction in the first eight chapters of Esther are translated into Ethiopic as follows:

(a) seventeen verb X + la-substantive Y + accusative substantive Z
(b) sixteen verb X + la-substantive Y + object clause Z
(c) fifteen verb X-suffix Y + accusative substantive Z
(d) eleven verb X-suffix Y + object clause Z
(e) three verb X + la-suffix Y + la-substantive Y + accusative substantive Z
(f) four verb X + la-suffix Y + accusative substantive Z
(g) two verb X-suffix Z + la-substantive Y
(h) one verb X-suffix Z + la-suffix Y
(i) one verb XZ + accusative substantive Y
(j) one verb XZ-suffix + la-substantive Y
(k) one verb XZ-suffix Y
(l) three verb X + preposition + substantive Y + accusative substantive Z
(m) two verb X + la-substantive Y + adverb.

The presence of a strict Greek-case equivalency for any of the Ethiopic object-forms seems most unlikely in view of the fact that any one of the latter -- accusative case, suffix, *la*-substantive, etc. -- may under given circumstances translate any of the Greek oblique cases.[12]

However, a tendency of the dative to translate as the analytic complement does appear in translation construction (h) (2:7):

en de tǭ metallaksai autēs	*wa'emdexra waḍ'at*
tous goneis	*emna azmādihā*
epaideusen autēn heautǭ	*ḫadanā lotu*
eis gunaika.	*tekuno be'esito*.
"When she lost her	"When she left
parents,	her family,
he brought her up	he brought her up
to be his wife."	to be his wife."

In this sentence, either object could have been translated by the suffix, either could have been translated by *la*- with the suffix.[13] But it was the dative object that actually received this translation.

Again, since all the Ethiopic object forms are attested as translations of the dative and the accusative when these occur alone (see below, B, C), some explanation is required for the predominance of translation constructions (a) and (b) when the dative and accusative occur together as, e.g., in 1:9 and 3:4,

Astin hē basilissa	*astin negešt*
epoiēsen poton	*gabrat ba'āla*
tais gunaiksin;	*la'anest*
"Vashti the queen	"Vashti the queen
had a party	had a party
for the women";	for the women";
hupedeiksan tǭ Aman	*nagarewwo lahāmā*
Mardokhaion tois tou basi-	*kama ya'abi mardokēwos*
leōs logois antitassomenon;	*te'ezzāza neguš;*
"They indicated to Haman	"They told Haman that Mordecai

that Mordecai was resisting	was resisting
the orders of the king."	the command of the king."

Why is construction (a) never reversed with the Greek dative object going to the Ethiopic synthetic complement and the Greek accusative to an Ethiopic la-form? Why are double synthetic or double analytic complements not attested? When the direct object is a clause (d) or a pronoun (g), why does the dative never translate as an Ethiopic accusative? When the dative object is a pronoun (c), why is the direct object never expressed with la-? For one reason or other, the Greek dative seems to be associated with the Ethiopic analytic complement.

We would suggest that this association is secondary. The Bible is full of reported speech: "And God said to Moses, 'Say to the people...'" etc. In the Greek Bible, this reported speech will almost always include a dative, the latter almost always a person. If the analytic complement originally carried an animation value, then it would normally -- or at least very frequently -- be used to translate these personal datives. And by dint of repetition, tne analytic complement could come to be associated with the case itself rather than with the case in a specific usage.

Once this secondary association was made, a three step development would begin. In the first step, from the translator's point of view, the analytic complement would be an acceptable translation of inanimate objects, as long as they were in the dative. In the second step, from the translation reader or hearer's point of view, the de facto use of the analytic complement with an inanimate object would mean that the analytic complement was now available for inanimate objects generally; i.e., because the restriction to the dative would be invisible in the Ethiopic itself. In the third step, this blurring of distinctions by the readers and hearers of the translation would rebound back into translation usage; the analytic complement, once available for non-personal objects only if they were dative, would now become available for the same non-personal objects even when they were accusative.

Retracing the development, we find in the first step that the animate/inanimate parameter is operative in Ethiopic but not in Greek, while the dative/accusative parameter is operative in Greek but not in Ethiopic. The two parameters do not harmonize: they are not part of the same system. The translator has to respect a parameter native to Ethiopic while finding ways to reflect one he finds in Greek. The result, in the second step, is a partial re-distribution of the two main forms of the complement to the verb along a parameter of independence or emphasis, an imitation of the dative/accusative parameter.

Schneider writes (without systematic consideration of any Greek Vorlagen):

> Si on examine d'une part les exemples de constructions synthétiques avec valeur déterminée de l'autre les exemples de la construction analytique, on remarque que ces derniers comportent généralement en plus une valeur insistante, une mise en relief du nom. ... Mais il ne faut pas oublier qu'il reste possible de traduire une nuance expressive et insistante par une tournure synthétique. Les cas les plus nets se trouvent avec l'accusatif (p. 71).

The "valeur insistante" that Schneider sees in the analytic complement is precisely the value we might expect from its association with the Greek dative, for the dative -- as the optional object -- has greater independence than the accusative. edōken timēn could be bracketed as a quantity: the transitive verb requires the accusative object and the accusative object the transitive verb. The same could not be said of edōken autǭ or edōken timēn autǭ. The dative is not required; and so, when it does occur, it stands in greater relief.[14]

However, even supposing that emphasis has indeed been introduced as a value carried by the analytic verbal component, we must doubt that it has systematically replaced the old value. The fact that "il reste possible de traduire une nuance expressive et insistante par une tournure synthétique" might not of itself exclude such regularity. We may easily enough suppose a distribution in which the synthetic complement is used whether or not the object is to be emphasized, the analytic complement only when it is to be emphasized. However, the fact that "les cas les plus nets se trouvent avec l'accusatif" must give us more pause. One of Schneider's examples from the Book of Esther is the following (3:11):

wayebēlo neguš lahāmā	"And the king said to Haman,
warq-sa yekunka laka wa-	'Let the gold be yours,
ḥezba-ni gebar zakama faqadka.	and as for the people, do
	as you will.'"

It would appear then that the third step in the development did not quite carry through. The new symmetry, in which Greek dative --> analytic complement = independence and emphasis, Greek accusative --> synthetic complement = dependence and lack of emphasis, was never perfectly established. Conversely, the old symmetry was never abolished to a point where all preference of personal and animate complements for the analytic complement would be obliterated. The present pattern of usage suggests rather a situation in which Greek influence has disrupted the native Ethiopic animation parameter but has not systematically replaced it.

That disruption and inconsistency should be the end result is hardly surprising, for the formal distinctions of any language simply cannot be maintained without the forms of that language. The dative/accusative distinction of Greek could not be brought into Ethiopic without the dative and without the accusative. It is not surprising either that a critic like Schneider can chart the attested uses of the analytic and the synthetic complements without quite catching what the Ethiopic writer is driving at: what the writer is driving at is not there in the Ethiopic to be caught. What Schneider's study produces, in all likelihood, is an image of the confusion in the "monoglot" Ethiopian's mind as he heard these translations read.

Translators tend to translate for other translators, and the distortions in Ethiopic were not so unmotivated that an Ethiopian who knew Greek could not feel the Greek behind the Ethiopic, just as we might feel the German through a sentence like:

> The world-relationship which runs through all the

> sciences as such constrains them to seek what-is *in itself*, with a view to rendering it, according to its quiddity (*Wasgehalt*) and its modality (*Seinsart*), an object of investigation and definition.[15]

However, to a reader who did not know German, the distortions of this sentence would feel like nothing in particular. If he should learn to write from such English, under what circumstances and how often would he write "*what*-finite verb" in place of "*that which* + finite verb"? The answer is: potentially, under any circumstances; but probably, seldom. A knowledge of the German translator's very specific motive for using the expression would tend to limit its use. Lacking a knowledge of German, the English writer is potentially free to use the expression anywhere. In practice, however, it is so un-English that he will avoid it.

Similarly in Ethiopic, to those many readers or hearers who did not know Greek or knew it impefectly, the distortions of translation felt like nothing in particular. They could not maintain the re-interpretation of forms begun by the translator, for they lacked the principle of his re-interpretation.

Two general objections to our analysis may be considered before we turn to the remaining translation constructions of IV,A.

First, the language of Ethiopic Esther is alleged to be the term of a development that begins with a translation from Greek. But the Bible was the first translation from Greek to Ethiopic. Therefore no development could have taken place before Esther.

The objection loses much of its force when one recalls that the translation of the Bible into Ethiopic is not only the first major translation into that language but also its first major literary monument of any sort. There was no standard literary Ethiopic to contrast with "Septuagint Ethiopic." Peculiarities introduced with the translation would have won immediate acceptance as the peculiarities of writing itself, of written language as opposed to spoken. They may even to an extent have been cultivated as the mark of literacy -- like Latinate grammar in Augustan England. The analysis of the complements does require that Esther not be the very first book translated from Greek to Ethiopic, but it does not require a very long interval between the translation of the first book and the translation of Esther. And we must leave open the possibility that the language of Esther has changed in its transmission; in other words, that the language of the surviving Ethiopic Esther mss. is the term of a development that began with the language of the first Ethiopic Esther ms.

Second, a query might be raised at the fact that no reinterpretation or redistribution of complements takes place after the substantive. The analytic complement after the substantive is identical to that after the verb. Why is it not affected?

No redistribution took place in the complements to the Ethiopic substantive because only one case, the genitive, is commonly used after the Greek substantive. A disruption and redistribution parallel to that of the complement to the verb could only have taken place if two cases were commonly used after the Greek substantive, just as two are used after the Greek verb. The two would have to distribute along some parameter other than animation, and some attempt would have to be made to reflect this parameter in Ethiopic. Conversely, since from the Greek end, the Ethiopic analytic/synthetic distribution in the noun complement is gratuitous (either form would do for the Greek meaning), we may presume that the distribution is native to Ethiopic. And since it is native, it must be regarded as originally common to all occurrences of the analytic/synthetic forms in Ethiopic; scil., also to the complements on the verb.[16]

Returning now to the remaining constructions of IV,A, we may consider first

(e, f). The three occurrences of (e) and the four of (f) are translations employing a small but significant number of Ethiopic verbs which, in Dillmann's terminology, do not take the double accusative and, in our own, do not take an animate object except after la-. They include, in examples from the Book of

Esther, *ṣahafa*, *sagada*, *gabra*, *naṣafa*, *gannaya*, and *ta'azzaza*; e.g. (6:3, E:21):

Tina doksan ē kharin epoiēsamen tō̧ Mardokhaiō̧?	*ay kebr waṣagā zagabarna lotu lamardokēwos.*
"What honor or favor did we do for Mordecai?"	"What honor and favor did we do for him, for Mordecai?"
epoiēsen autois euphrosunen	*gabra lomu tefšeḥta*
"He made joy for them."	"He made joy for them."

Why are the forms *gabarnāhu lamardokēwos* and *gabromu tefšeḥta* not used? The verb is not incapable of taking the suffix. Cf. 5:8,

aurion poiēso ta auta.	*gēšama egbaro.*
"Tomorrow I shall do it."	"Tomorrow I shall do it."

Nor, as we have seen, is the suffix incapable of replacing a personal object. Cf. 5:11,

hupedeiksen autois ton plouton autou	*ar'ayomu be'lo.*
"He showed them his wealth."	"He showed them his wealth."

Synchronically, the insertion of *la*- before the suffix may be regarded as a lexical peculiarity. Diachronically, it may either be a lexical peculiarity -- that is, the verbs in question may be the survival of a verb class -- or it may be the dative = *la*-association of which we have spoken occurring in a more pronounced form after verbs with which the dative is unusually common. (Cf. below note 16.)

(*i, j, k*). In these three constructions, the complement Z disappears as a distinct word because it is included in the Ethiopic verb: *peritithenai timēn* = *akbara* (1:20), *didonai domata* + *faṭaṭa* (A:16), *epibalein kheiras* = *gaṭala* (A:16); e.g. (1:20),

pasai hai gunaikes	*kwellon anest*

perithēsousin timēn	yākaberā
tois andrasin heautōn.	amtātihon.
"All the women	"All the women
will give honor	will honor
to their husbands."	their husbands."

(l). The three occurrences of (l) also have ad hoc lexical explanations: aphairein = naš'a em (8:2), kakian poiein = gabra ekiyta la'ela (8:3), kheiras epipherein = anše'a eda la'ela (8:8); e.g. (8:2),

ton daktulion	ḫelqata
hon apheilato Aman.	zanaš'a em'eda hāmā.
"The ring	"The ring
which he took from Haman."	which he took from the hand of Haman."

(m). The two occurrences of (m) are translations using kamaze for the anticipatory demonstrative tade; e.g. (B:1),

tois ... toparkhais	lamasāfent...
tade graphei.	kamaze ṣaḫafa.
"To the local authorities	"To the authorities
he writes thus."	he writes thus."

B. Greek active verb X + dative object Y used alone. In the first eight chapters of Esther, seventy occurrences of this construction are translated into Ethiopic as follows;

(a) twenty-five verb X-suffix + la-substantive Y
(b) four verb X + accusative substantive Y
(c) fourteen verb X-suffix Y
(d) four verb X + la-suffix Y
(e) two verb X-suffix Y + la-suffix Y
(f) three verb X-suffix + la-suffix Y + la-substantive Y
(g) six verb X + la-substantive Y
(h) one verb X + nominative Y + subjunctive

(i) nine verb X + preposition + substantive Y
(j) one preposition X + substantive Y
(k) one preposition X-suffix Y.

(a). Construction (a) is the most common translation of Greek verb X + dative substantive Y. One notes that in every case, Y is personal; e.g. (4:8),

lalēson tǭ basilei.	negreyo'a laneguš'a
"Say to the king."	"Say to the king."

(b). In two of the four occurrences of (b), Y is non-personal; in two it is ḥezb; e.g. (3:11),

tǭ de ethnei	ḥezba-ni
khrō hōs boulei	gebar zakama faqadka.
"Treat the people	"As for the people,
as you wish."	do as you will."

(c). The occurrences of construction (c) all translate Greek active verb X + dative pronoun Y; e.g. (3:4),

kath hekastēn hēmeran	kwello amira
elaloun autǭ.	yebēlewwo.
"Every day	"Every day
they spoke to him."	they spoke to him."

(d, e, f). The occurrences of (d) and (e) also translate Greek X + dative pronoun Y. The variation from (c) may be the survival of a verb class, or it may be simply the result of the la- = dative association; e.g. (3:5, 5:13),

ou proskunei autǭ Mardokhaios;	iyesaged lotu mardokēwos;
"Mordecai does not bow down to him";	"Mordecai does not bow down to him";
tauta moi ouk areskei.	lita-sa iyehēwezani zentu.
"This does not please me."	"This does not please me."

The repetition of la- in the occurrences of (f) probably is not be explained in the same way (cf. above, p. 49); e.g. (C:25, 6:10),

boēthēson moi tę̄ monę̄;	red'ani lita labaḥtāwit;

"Help me who am alone";	"Help me who am alone"'
houtōs estai panti anthrōpǭ hon ho basileus doksazei.	*kamaze yekawen lotu labe'esi zaneguš akbaro.*
"Thus it will be for every man whom the king honors."	"Thus it will be for the man whom the king honors."

(g). The six occurrences of construction (g) are dative noun objects of *graphein* and *epitassein*. These verbs are translated by *ṣaḫafa* and *azzaza* from the class of verbs spoken of above (IV, A, f and IV, B, d-f); e.g. (3:12),

hōs epetaksen Aman tois stratēgois	*bakama azzaza hāmā lamalā'ekt*
"As Haman commanded the generals."	"As Haman commanded the generals."

(h). the one occurrence of (h) translates a Greek impersonal verb with an infinitive complement. In the Ethiopic, the dative object of X becomes the subject of a complement subjunctive; scil. (3:8),

ou sumpherei tǭ basilei easai autous.	*ikona retu' yāḫdegomu neguš.*
"It is not profitable for the king to tolerate them."	"It is not right that the king should tolerate them."

(i). The occurrences of (i) translate Greek verbs with prepositional prefixes: *proserkhesthai* = *maṣ'a xaba* (1:14), *sumpiein* + *maṣḥa mesla*, etc.: e.g. (4:5)

ton eunoukhon autēs hos pareistēkei autę̄.	*xeṣwa zayeqawem qedmēhā.*
"Her eunuch who was standing by her."	"Her eunuch who was standing before her."

(j). In the one occurrence of (j), X is *deutereuein*, which has no verbal equivalent in Ethiopic and must be translated by a preposition; scil. (4:8),

ho deutereuōn tǭ basilei.	*za'emtaḫta'a neguš'a*

"The man second to the king."	"He who is below the king."

(k). Here an already semiticized Greek idiom for possession receives its idiomatic Ethiopic expression (2:7):

en toutọ pais.	botu walata.
"He had a child."	"He had a daughter."

C. Greek passive verb + dative object.

1. Greek passive impersonal verb X + dative object Y. In the first eight chapters of the Book of Esther, a single occurrence of this construction is translated into Ethiopic by indicative active X + object clause + la-substantive Y.

The impersonal proleptic character of the Greek passive impersonal construction would not be retained by the most mechanical Ethiopic translation. Mechanically, we would translate (3:14):

kai prosetagē pasin tois ethnesin hetoimous einai eis tēn hēmeran tautēn.	ta'azzaza lakwellu aḥzāb kama yekunu, etc.
"And it was commanded to all the peoples to be ready on that day."	"And it was commanded to all the peoples that they should be," etc.

However. in Ethiopic it is the third plural active rather than the passive of the t-form which is used when a personal construction is impossible. And from the present example it would appear that the Ethiopic only resorts to the third plural when the subject is actually unknown: if a subject can be supplied from the context, a personal construction will be used; scil., in 3:14, where the subject is known to be Haman,

"He commanded all the proples that they should be there on that day."	azzaza lakwellu aḥzab kama yekunu lawe'etu 'elat.

2. Greek third person passive imperative X + dative object Y. In the first eight chapters of the Book of Esther, two occurrences of this construction are translated as follows:
   (a) one active subjunctive X-suffix + *la*-substantive Y
   (b) one active subjunctive X + accusative substantive + *la*-substantive Y.

When an Ethiopic *t*-form has a genuinely passive meaning, the form is not used in the imperative. *t*-form imperatives occur only when the meaning of the form is resultative-middle. Since both the Greek verbs to be translated here are genuine passives, the Ethiopic has to shift to the active.

The subject of the passive imperative becomes the direct object of the Ethiopic subjunctive with the dative object retained as a suffix or a *la*-substantive in the various combinations listed above (IV, B). The two examples given here are (2:2, 2:3):

zētēthētō tō̜ basilei korasia aphthora;	*yexšešu laneguš awāleda danāgela;*
"Let beautiful girls be sought for the king";	"Let them seek for the king virgins";
paradothētōsan tō̜ eunoukhō̜ tou basileōs.	*wayāwfeyewwon laxeṣwa neguš.*
"Let them be given to the king's eunuch."	"Let them hand them over to the king's eunuch."

3. Greek passive indicative X + dative object Y. In the first eight chapters of the book of Esther, three occurrences of this construction are translated as follows:
   (a) one passive indicative X + *emxaba* + substantive Y
   (b) one passive indicative X + *la*-suffix Y
   (c) one passive indicative X + *la*-substantive Y;

scil. (B:3,E;3, 7:10),

tēn pothoumenēn	salāma
tois pasin anthrōpois	za'emxaba kwellu sabe'
eirēnēn;	yetfaqar;
"Peace, desired of all men";	"Peace, which by all men is desired";
tous hupotetagmenous hēmin;	ella yetkwēnanu lana'
"Those subordinate to us";	"Those who are under our jurisdiction";
epi tou ksulou ho hētoimasthē Mardokhaiō.	diba we'etu 'ed za'astaḍalawa lamardokēwos.
"Upon the gibbet that was prepared for Mordecai."	"Upon the gibbet that was prepared for Mordecai."

D. Greek verb X + adverbial dative Y. Fifteen occurrences of this construction are translated into Ethiopic as follows: verb X + ba-substantive Y. All fifteen occurrences translate datives of means or manner; e.g. (8:3),

sphragisate tō daktuliō mou.	yeḥtemu bamāxetameya
"Stamp it with my signet."	"Let them stamp it with my signet."

E. Greek verb X + accusative Y used alone. In the first eight chapters of Esther, two-hundred-eight occurrences of this construction are translated into Ethiopic as follows:

(a) ninety-seven verb X + accusative substantive Y
(b) fifty verb X-suffix + la-substantive Y
(c) thirty-three verb X-suffix Y
(d) three verb X-suffix Y + kiya-suffix Y
(e) three verb X + la-substantive Y
(f) one verb X + la-suffix Y + la-substantive Y
(g) one verb X + substantive Y

(h) twelve verb X + preposition + substantive Y

(i) seven nominative Y + verb X

(j) one verb XY.

(a). Of the ninety-seven occurrences of (a), eighty-eight are non-personal, e.g. (4:1),

deierreksen ta himtia heautou;	šaṭaṭa albāsihu;
"He tore his clothes";	"He tore his clothes";

while nine are personal, e.g. (1:18),

tolmēsousin homoiōs atimasai tous andras autōn.	kamāhu yetxabalā emantu-ni amtātihon yāstaḥagerā.
"They will dare similarly to dishonor their husbands."	"Thus they will dare to dishonor their husbands."

(b.) Of the fifty occurrences of (b), forty-four are personal, e.g. (1:11),

eisagagein tēn basilissan;	kama yāmṣe'ewwā lanegešt;
"To lead in the queen";	"To bring the queen";

while six are non-personal, e.g. (2:18),

hupsōsen tous gamous Esthēr.	a'bayo lamāre'a astēr.
"He turned Esther's wedding into a great affair."	"He turned Esther's wedding into a great affair."

(c). All the occurrences of (c) translate Greek verb X + accusative prounoun Y; e.g. (2:2),

kai hōs katekrinen autēn.	wa'emdexra kwannanā.
"And as he judged her."	"And after he judged her."

(d). The occurrences of (d) translate the same construction where the pronoun comes before the verb. Contrast 4:8 and C:25:

kai hrusai hēmas ek thanatou;	wa'adxenena'a emmot'a
"And save us from death";	"And save us from death";
hēmas de hrusai en kheiri sou.	wakiyana-sa adxenama ba'edēka.
"Save us by your hand."	"Save us by your hand."

In all the occurrences of (c) that are not relative clauses, the accusative pronoun comes after the verb. In all the occurrences of (d), the pronoun comes before the verb. In these facts, we have probably the answer to the question why the problem of translating datives and accusatives into Ethiopic was not solved -- at least for pronouns -- by using la- for the dative and kiya- for the accusative. Either the translator wanted to reflect the Greek word order where he could, or he felt that kiya- -- meaning often ipse, idem, rather than is[17] -- was too strong for the Greek personal prounoun or autos in the accusative.

(e, f). Cf. above p. 47. An example (C:5):

to mē proskunein	kama iyesgod
ton huperēphanon Aman.	la'ebd hāmā.
"Not bowing down	"That I would not bow down
to the proud Haman."	to the slave Haman."

The occurrences of these forms as translations of the accusative rather than the dative argue the more strongly that they constitute an original class.

(g). The complement Y in this construction is egzi'abḥēr. With this complement, especially when the verb is farha, it is clear from context that an accusative is intended; scil., (2:20),

phobeisthai ton theon.	kama tefran egzi'abḥēr.
"To fear God."	"That you fear God."

(h). The twelve occurrences of (h) have as a lexical peculiarity that they may -- and perhaps in the present translator always do -- take a preposition before the direct object: epikalein = sa'la xaba, phobeisthai = farha emna, adikein = 'abbasa lā'ela, etc.; e.g. (C:13),

spodou kai kopriōn	marēta waḥamada
eplēsen tēn kephalēn autēs.	mal'at westa re'esā.
"She covered her head	"She covered her head
with ash and dust."	with dust and ash."

(i). Of the seven occurrences of (i), four translate Greek accusative + infinitive constructions; e.g. (2:15),

en de tō anaplerousthai ton khronon Esthēr.	wa'ama baṣḥa 'elata ebrētā la'astēr.
"When Esther's time came."	"When Esther's time came."

Another two occurrences translate the Greek ekhein + accusative by the Ethiopic idiom for possession, kona + suffix. In the remaining occurrence, we find another idiomatic translation (2:15):

ēn gar Esthēr heuriskousa kharin.	bāti mogas la'astēr.
"Esther found favor."	"Esther had favor."

(j). In the one occurrence of this construction, the Ethiopic verb alone carries the meaning of the Greek verb + substantive; scil. (3:7),

kai ebaien klērous.	wa'asta'aṣawa.
"He cast lots."	"He cast lots."

F. Greek verb + preposition + substantive.

1. Greek verb X + preposition + substantive Y. Two-hundred-thirty-one occurrences of this construction in the first eight chapters of Esther are translated into Ethiopic as follows:
   - (a) two-hundred-twenty-two verb X + preposition + substantive Y
   - (b) six verb X + subjunctive Y + direct object
   - (c) three verb X-suffix Y + la-substantive Y.

(a). Construction (a) is plainly the mechanical equivalent of the Greek; e.g., (8:3),

kai katestēsen Esthēr Mardokhaion epi pantōn tōn Aman.	wasēmato astēr lamardokēwos lā'ela kwellu zahāmā.
"And Esther set Mordecai over everything of Haman's."	"And Esther set Mordecai over everything of Haman's."

(b). This construction translates the Greek use of eis or pros + accusative to express purpose; e.g. (2:7),

epaideusen autēn heautō̧ eis gunaika.	ḫadanā lotu tekuno be'esito.
"He brought her up to be his wife."	"He brought her up to be his wife."

(c). This construction translates Greek pros + accusative used in place of the dative; e.g. (5:6),

en de tō̧ potō̧ eipen ho basileus pros Esthēr.	bawesta ba'āl yebēlā neguš la'astēr.
"At the banquet the king said to Esther."	"At the banquet the king said to Esther."

2. Greek passive verb X + preposition + agent Y. Six occurrences of this construction in the first eight chapters of Esther are translated into Ethiopic as follows:
   (a) three construct substantive X + substantive Y
   (b) three nominative substantive Y + verb X + object.

In Ethiopic, as elsewhere in Semitic, the agent of a passive verb is not normally expressed. Where Greek does express it, Ethiopic will shift to a nominal expression or to an active verb.

(a). The nominal expression is used when the Greek names the agent but not the dative object of the action; e.g. (8:14),

ta hupo tou basileōs legomena. te'ezzāza negu.
"The things said by the king." "The command of the king."

The Greek does not indicate to whom the speech was addressed. If it did, the Ethiopic could not have fitted that indication into the construct.

(b). Under such a circumstance, an active transformation would have been necessary; e.g. (1:18),

ta tō basilei lekhthenta hup autēs.	zakama tawa'ato laneguš.
"The things said by her to the king."	"How she contradicted the king."

G. Greek verb X + genitive substantive Y. In the first eight chapters of the Book of Esther, seventeen occurrences of this construction are translated into Ethiopic as follows:

(a) nine verb X + accusative substantive Y
(b) one verb X-suffix + la-substantive Y
(c) one verb X + la-substantive Y
(d) six verb X + preposition + substantive Y.

The translation constructions divide much as those of the accusative.

(a). E.g., (B:2, 4:8),

pollōn eparksas ethnōn;	bezuxa aḫzāba kwannineya;
"Ruling many nations";	"Judging many nations";
mnēstheisa hēmerōn.	tazkāri'a mawā'ela'a.
"Recalling the days."	"Recalling the days."[18]

(b). E.g. (2:1),

ouketi emnēsthē tēs Astin.	itazakkarā enka la'astin
"He no longer remembered Vashti."	"Then he did not remember Vashti."

(c). E.g. (3:8),

tōn de nomōn tou basileōs parakouousin.	iyet'ēzazu laḫega neguš
"They disobey the laws of the king."	"They disobey the law of the king."

Cf. above, p. ...

(d). E.g. (3:1),

hupsōsen auton kai eprōtobathrei pantōn tōn philōn autou.	wa'anbaro lā'ela emna kwellu a'rektihu.

"He raised him up and set him ahead of all his friends."	"He set him above all his friends."

V. ADJECTIVE-TO-SUBSTANTIVE SUBORDINATION: Greek substantive X + adjective Y. One-hundred-fifty-three occurrences of this construction in the first eight chapters of Esther are translated into Ethiopic as follows:

(a) one-hundred-thirteen substantive X + adjective Y
(b) eleven construct substantive X + noun Y
(c) twenty-two substantive X + za-Y
(d) three substantive X + noun Y
(e) two substantive X-suffix Y
(f) two substantive XY.

(a). Construction (a), which includes both genuine adjectives and suffixed nouns functioning as adjectives (e.g., kwell-, bāḥtit-), is plainly the mechanical equivalent of the Greek; e.g. (8:1, 2:9, 1:20, E:21),

kai en autē tē hemerą;	wabaye'eti 'elat;
"And on the same day";	"And on that day";
kai ta hepta korasia;	wasabe'u awāleda;
"And the seven girls";	"And the seven girls";
pasai hai gunaikes;	kwellon anest;
"All the women";	"All the women";
ant'olethrias tou eklektou genous.	heyanta mesnāhomu laḥezb ḥeruy.
"Instead of the destruction of the chosen people."	"Instead of the destruction of the chosen people."

In the remaining constructions, except construction (f), the adjective required for a mechanical translation is either not attested or is rare and not attested in the Bible (therefore probably late). The different constructions -- at least (b) and (c) -- seem to reflect refinements of conception which are not maintained in an adjectival translation and must increasingly have been lost as the use of the adjective spread in Ethiopic. However, the value of formal equivalence with the Greek was more clearly in the mind of the translator than any other stylistic consideration.

(f). The four occurrences of (f) are Ethiopic substantives translating Greek substantives + adjective; e.g. (6:8),

stolēn bussinēn	mēlata
hēn ho basileus periballetai.	zayelabes neguš.
"The purple cloak	"The purple
which the king wears."[19]	which the king wears."

(e). The two occurrences of (e) are pronominal adjectives; e.g. (E:10),

allotrios...tēs hēmeteras	rehuq...
khrēstotētos.	emxirutena.
"Foreign...	"Far...
to our virtue."	from our virtue."

(d). Two or the three occurrences of (d) are apposition; e.g. (2:3),

epileksatōsan	yexrayu lotu
korasia parthenika.	awāleda danāgela.
"Let them choose	"Let them choose
virgins."	virgins."

The third is a nominal sentence; scil. (D:14),

thaumastos ei, kurie.	madmem anta, egzi'o.
"You are wonderful, Lord."	"You are a wouder, God."

The nominal sentence would appear to be a distinct translation pattern: Greek adjective + einai --> Ethiopic noun + pronoun. However, the apposition is formally close enough to the relative clause to be considered a special instance of it; i.e., where the relative clause expresses apposition, the relative marker may be dropped. awāleda zadanāgel we'eton has the same meaning as awāleda danāgela, and the two may be considered as opposed in somewhat the same way to a construct like awāleda dengelnā* ("daughters of virginity").

(b, c). The main distinction among the non-adjectival translations es that between the construct phrase and the relative clause. Here aqain, however, any semantic distinction between the two is clouded by formal exigencies. Specifically, when the Greek adjective cannot be represented by an Ethiopic noun but only by a verb or a phrase, then the Ethiopic relative must be used; e.g. (1:8, 1:19),

oinos polus kai hēdus;	*wayn bezux zašannay mā'azāhu;*
"Wine abundant and sweet";	"Much wine which had a delicious taste."
gunaiki kreittoni autēs.	*be'esit enta texēyesa.*
"A woman better than she."	"A woman who surpassed her."

Since thirteen of the twenty-two occurrences of (c) are of this sort, the semantic contrast with (b) can only be traced in nine occurrences. Of these, eight are phrases giving the material from which a thing is made, e.g. (1:7),

potēria khrusa kai argura.	*ṣewā'āt-ni zawarq wazaberur.*
"Golden and silver cups."	"Golden and silver cups."

The remaining occurrence is (B:5):

tode to ethnos monotaton.	*zentu ḥezb feluṭ enta bāhtitu.*
"This most solitary people."	"This segregated solitary people."

Of the occurrences of (b), five are the equivalent of the *zawarq* of (c); e.g. (8:15),

stephanon ekhōn khrusoun.	*zabo aklila warq.*
"Having a golden crown."	"Having a gold crown."

The remaining six occurrences are the following (1:6, 2:12, 2:17, 5:4, E:16, 8:15):

parinou lithou;	*ebna parinu*
"Mother-of-pearl stone";	"Mother-of-pearl stone";
smurninọ elaiọ;	*qebe'a 'efrat;*
"Myrrh oil";	"Myrrh oil";
to diadema to gunaikeion;	*aklila anest;*
"The women's crown";	"The women's crown";
Hēmera...episēmos;	*'elata ba'āl;*
"Feast day";	"Feast day";
en tẹ̄ kallistẹ̄ diathesei;	*basenna lebbena;*

"In fairest sentiment";	"In fair sentiment";
basilikēn stolēn	albāsa mangeśt.
"Royal cloak."	"Royal vesture."

Is there a semantic difference between (b) and (c), between X-a + Y and X + za-Y? With some hesitation, we suggest that when (b) is used, the phrase carries the nuance of two objects in relationship; when (c) is used, the nuance is that of a single object with one of its qualities abstracted. In other words, in X-a + Y, the particularity of Y is preserved; in X + za-Y it is lost.

Is there a difference in English between "a gold crown" and "a golden crown"? Not much, surely, and the distinction can hardly be central since it is not carefully maintained; cf. "a silver crown." And yet to the extent that a distinction is present, we must look for it in the fact that the phrase "a gold crown" names the metal by its own name. The material from which the product is made is present in its own right: "golden" is not a thing, "gold" is.[20]

Or again, is there a difference between "biblical wisdom" and "Bible wisdom"? If there is, it would be the difference between the wisdom of Ecclesiastes and the wisdom of Billy Graham. The Bible is not present as a book, as a thing in its own right, in Ecclesiastes' biblical wisdom. The Bible is present as a thing in its own right in Billy Graham's Bible wisdom. Biblical wisdom is a kind of wisdom. Bible wisdom is an action using a book.

Obviously, the English contrast of adjective with adjectivized noun is most closely paralleled by the Ethiopic contrast of adjective with construent noun (as mangeśt in albāsa mangeśt). We would suggest, however, that within Ethiopic the contrast between adjective and construent noun and the contrast between za-noun and construent noun are close to being the same contrast. In other words, of the two constructions that are not formally adjectival, the za-noun construction is more nearly the semantic equivalent of the adjective. It is then equally the adjective/construent noun contrast and the za-noun/construent noun contrast that may be compared to the English contrast between adjective and adjectivized noun.

Dillmann refers to za- as "nota genitivi" (Lexicon, col. 1031; cf. Grammatik, p. 290). However, the meaning of the za-noun construction is perhaps more accurately caught in some of his more specific observations; e.g., (Lexicon, col. 1032), "substantivis materiae praepositum adjectiva materiae efficit" and "Crebro... is qui est alcjs i.e. pertinens ad algm vel algd, praeditus, possidens." In Amharic, the adjectival use of the za-noun construction became extremely common. Even in Ethiopic, the construction is frequently placed before the noun it modifies; e.g., (Matthew 8:10),[21]

irakabku	"I have not found
zamaṭanaze hāymānot.	a faith as great as this."

These facts, on the one hand, and, on the other, the fact that the construction almost never translates the Greek genitive but frequently translates the Greek adjective make its adjectival character clear.

The question that must be asked is why, if the za-noun construction is semantically so close to the adjective, it is not always used when a given Greek adjective cannot be translated by an Ethiopic adjective.

In answering, we may look first at some of the Greek adjectives of (b) and at our English translations. Why, for example, is to diadema to gunaikeion "the women's crown" and not "the feminine crown"? We have spoken of the difference between two objects in relation and one object with a quality abstracted. But either point of view may be taken in almost any situation. Can a quality like femininity inhere in, and so be abstracted from, an object like a crown? The Greek answer seems to be Yes, the English answer No. With sufficient reflection, either answer can be made to seem plausible.

Similarly then in Ethiopic, once the initial bias towards a formal translation is neutralized -- i.e., when the formal correspondent, an Ethiopic adjective, is unavailable, then the language translates adjectivally, where, habitually, it "thinks" adjectivally and does not where it does not. In the long run, the choice of one construction over the other is apt to be only a weighted either/or; i.e., there is most likely only a lexically determined statistical preference of one construction over another for a given pair of Ethiopic nouns. Such preferences can only be determined a posteriori; and since they are lexically determined, they are far more subject to extra-linguistic influence than syntax. In German, the English and the Italians are not die Englischen and die Italienischen but die Engländer and die Italiener; the Germans, however, are not die Deutschländer but die Deutschen. The reality spoken of does not impose the conception, rather the conception is imposed upon the reality.

VI. SUBSTANTIVE-TO-ADJECTIVE SUBORDINATION.

The predictability in translation of substantives subordinated to Greek adjectives depends on the predictability in translation of the adjectives themselves. Only if the adjective translates as an adjective, can the construction of its substantive complement be predicted.

A. Greek substantive X + adjective Y + complement Z, where an Ethiopic adjective Y is available. In the first eight chapters of Esther, five occurrences of this construction are translated as follows: substantive X + adjective Y + accusative substantive Z; e.g., (D:14),

kai to prosōpon sou kharitōn meston.	wagaṣṣeka melu' mogasa.
"And your face was full of love."	"And your face was full of grace."

B. Greek substantive X + adjective Y + preposition + substantive Z, where an Ethiopic adjective Y is available. Five occurrences of this construction in the first eight chapters of Esther are translated as follows: substantive X + adjective Y + preposition + substantive Z; e.g., (3:8),

hoi de nomoi autōn eksalloi para panta ta ethnē.	waḥegomu-ni kāle' emna kwellu aḥzāb.
"Their laws are different from all peoples."	"Their laws are different from all peoples."

VII. COORDINATION OF SENTENCES.

Greek sentences in the first eight chapters of Esther, where coordinated, are coordinated by conjunctions (kai, oun, gar), particles (de, etc.), and adverbs (houtos, etc.). In every case but one, Ethiopic translates by conjunctions (wa, etc.), particles (-sa, -ni, etc.), and adverbs (kamahu, etc.), sometimes using a conjunction where Greek has a particle or vice-versa, but always maintaining coordination where Greek has coordination. The exception to this rule is Greek gar + coordinated sentence which is translated into Ethiopic by esma + subordinate clause.

VIII. FORMULAIC LANGUAGE.

By formulaic language in a translation, we understand language which though not reflecting the form of the original, is predictable in another way. Within the translation language, given forms of expression can be bound to given language situations in such a way that when the translator comes upon the situation in the original language, the form of his translation will be determined immediately and without reference to the form of the original. Thus we may translate "Les morts etaient mille neuf cents cinquante" as "The dead were one thousand nine hundred fifty," but "Il est mort en mille neuf cents cinquante" must be translated "He died in 1950 (nineteen fifty)." In the second mille neuf cents cinquante, what we might take from the French formally is blocked by the prior cue "This is a date." Once the cue is caught, the form of our English translation, even to the detail of its being written in numerals, is determined.

For reasons that will be explained, the study of the formulaic translation process has only a limited relevance to the study of the predictability of translation syntax. However, it may be useful to consider at least one example of it in some detail.

A. Date formulae in the first eight chapters of the Book of Esther.

1. Dating to day alone. A single occurrence is translated: ba-ordinal + ʿelat; scil. (1:10),

en de tē hēmera tē hebdomē.	wabasābeʿ ʿelat.
"On the seventh day."	"On the seventh day."

2. Dating to month alone. A single occurrence is translated: bawarex + za-ordinal + zasemu + month name; scil. (3:13),

aphanisai to genos tōn Ioudaiōn en hēmera mia mēnos	kama yātfeʾewwomu lazamada ayhud baʾaḥatti ʿelat bawarex

dōdekatou	za'asartu
hos estin Adar.	wakel'ētu azsemu adār.
"To destroy the nation of the Jews in one day of the twelfth month which is Adar."	"To destroy the nation of the Jews in one day of the twelfth month which is called Adar."

The phrase en mią hēmerą does not indicate the date of the genocide but its speed: the nation was to be destroyed in a single day. The Ethiopic expression for "first of the month" used eḥud, amir, or qadāmi but not aḥatti (Dillmann, Grammatik, p. 322 ff.), which is a cardinal, not an ordinal.[22] Effectively then bawarex, etc., is not part of a formula dating to a smaller unit than the month. Note that both the name and the number of the month are included.

3. Dating to year alone. Two occurrences are translated as follows:
   (a) ba-ordinal + 'am; scil. (1:3),

en tǭ tritǭ etei;	bašales 'ām;
"In the third year";	"In the third year"

   (b) ba-numerals +'amat; scil. (3:7),

en etei dōdekatǭ.	ba 10 wa 2 'āmat.
"In the twelfth year."	"In the twelfth year."

The variation 'am/'amat most likely has no significance. In view of the use of the ordinal in (a), the numerals in (b) should probably be read as ordinals: ba'ašartu wakāle't.

4. Dating to day of month. Four occurrences are translated as follows:
   (a) two ama + numerals + lašarqa + month name; e.g., (B:6),

tę̄ tessareskaidekatę̄	ama 10 wa 4
tou mēnos Adar;	lašarqa adār;
"The fourteenth of the month of Adar"'	"The fourteenth of the month of Adar";

(b) one day-of-month form[23] + lašarqa warexa + month name: (scil. (3:7),

kai epēsen ho klēros eis tēn tessareskaidekatēn tou mēnos, hos estin Adar; "And the lot fell to the fourteenth of the month of Adar";	wawarada 'eḏu lā'ela 'ašuru warabu'u lašarqa warexa adār; "And the lot fell to the fourteenth of the month of Adar";

(c) one ba-ordinal warex ama numerals lašarq; scil. (3:12),

mēni prōtǭ tę triskaidekatę. "In the first month on the thirteenth."	bagadāmi warex ama 10 wa 3 lašarq. "In the first month on the thirteenth."

Superficially, these three translations differ in several particulars, but perhaps they can be harmonized. First of all, we may assume that the numerals in (a) stand for day-of-month forms as found in (b). Secondly, since every šarq is a šarqa warex, we may assume that warex could have been added to (a) or dropped from (b); in other words, that it is an optional element. (b) is the complement of the verb warada + preposition lā'ela; were it not so used, we may assume that the ama of the other two occurrences would also be present in it.

The use of ba- in (c) would appear to be connected with the use of the number of the month (prōtǭ/qadāmi) instead of its name (Nisan/nisa). If the name were used, we would have ama 10 wa 3 lašarqa nisa and not bawarexa nisa ama 10 wa 3 lašarq.

5. Dating to month of year. A single occurence is translated: ba-numerals + awrāx + bawarexa + month name + ba-ordinal + 'ām; scil. (2:16),

tǭ dōdekatǭ mēni hos estin Adar tǭ hebdomǭ etei.	ba 10 wa 2 awrāx bawarexa adār basābe' 'ām.

"In the twelfth month	"In the 12th month
which is Adar	in the month of Adar
in the seventh year."	in the seventh year."

warex has a plural, awrāx, and a doubled plural, awrāxāt; but once awrāxāt has been coined, awrāx is available also as a singular.[24] In other words, bawarexa adār simply repeats ba 10 wa 2 awrāx, giving the name in place of the number.

6. Dating to day of month of year. A single example is translated ba-ordinal ʻāmat + ama-ordinal + za-month name; scil. (A:1)

etous deuterou	bakāle' ʻāmat
basileuontos artakserksou	emza nagša artakserksēs
tou megalou	ʻabiy
tę̄ mią tou Nisa.	ama qadāmit zanisa.
"In the second year	"In the second year
of the reign of Artaxerxes	of the reign of Artaxerxes
the great	the great
on the first of Nisan."	on the first of Nisan."

Here the year-formula and the use of ama in the month-formula agree with what we have just seen. However, in place of the day-of-month forms, we have an ordinal; and in place of lašarqa + month name, we have za- + month name. The variation may result from some peculiarities attending the first day of the month. That is, ama eḥud (or qadāmit) lašarqa nisa matches the other day-of-month constructions formally but is redundant in sense: the first of the kalends is the kalends itself. Either the number or lašarqa must be dropped. If the number were dropped, we would read ama šarqa nisa (cf. Dillmann, Lexicon, col. 239). As it is, lašarqa has been dropped and za, necessarily, added.

As noted above (p. 68) formulaic language in a translation is the correlation of a situation and a fixed form of expression not in the original language but in the translation language. If a situation and a form of expression are bound only in the original language, then the translation will not be formulaic but will be mechanical; i.e., it will attend to the syntactic components of the original expression and attempt to reproduce them with the nearest equivalents in the translation language. It is this process that we have been attempting to chart in what we have called the syntacticon.

If on the other hand the situation and the form of expression are bound in the translation language, then whether or not they are bound in the original, the translation will be formulaic; i.e., it will desregard the individual suntactic components of the original in the same way that the individual phonetic components of words are disregarded in a lexicon. And in this case the syntacticon becomes impossible. It becomes impossible, for it requires that the syntax of the original be available for imitation by the translation; but as noted above (p. 68), in situations where the translation language is formulaic, such imitation is blocked: a situation-cue from the original, not its syntax, determines the syntax of the translation.

Thus one will note that on the chart of date formulae below (p. 118), the input, the top half of the chart, is entirely situational, while on all the previous charts the input has been syntactic or syntactic and semantic. Again, on the same chart, questions are asked about the Greek phrase as a whole, not -- as in all the earlier charts -- about parts of the phrase, specific components that could be labeled X, Y, Z. The chart is useful as a way to parlay a few examples of Greek-Ethiopic date-translation into the equivalent of a page from a Greek-Ethiopic phrasebook by using the information from each example on all the other examples. However, to the study of the predictability of Ethiopic syntax in translations from the Greek, the chart is essentially irrelevant. It is relevant to note that in given situations, the syntax of the translation relates to the language-situation of the original rather than to its syntax. But to carry the matter further and describe precisely which formulae pattern with which situational cues must be conceived as a separate study, though one no less necessary than the study of free syntax to the task of rendering translation automatic.

Other examples of formulaic translation in the first four chapters of the Book of Esther may include the following:

B. *Time formulae other than dates.*

1. Duration: two occurrences of, e.g. (2:12),

mēnas hex aleiphomenai	*6 awrāx enza yetqābe'ā*
en smurninō elaiō kai	*qebe'a 'efrat*
mēnas hex en tois arōmasin.	*wa 6 awrāx ba'afawāt.*
"Anointed for six months with myrrh oil and for six months with perfumes."	"Anointed for six months with myrrh oil and for six months with perfumes."

2. Recurrence: two occurrences of, e.g. (3:7)

kai ebalen klerous	*wa'asta 'aṣawa*
hēmeran ex hēmeras.	*'elata em'elat.*
"And he cast lots daily."	"And he cast lots daily."

Two occurrences of, e.g. (2:11),

kath hekastēn de hēmeran	*wakwello amira*
ho Mardokhaios periepatei.	*yemaṣe' mardokēwos.*
"Every day Mordecai would walk."	"And every day Mordecai would go."

One occurrence (4:16) of,

nēsteusate...	*ṣumu'a...*
nukta kai hēmeran.	*ma'āleta'a walēlita'a.*
"Fast... night and day."	"Fast... day and night."

3. Miscellaneous temporal expressions: "at dawn, at dusk" (2:14),

deilēs eisporeuetai	wafenā sark tebawe'
kai pros hēmeran apotrekhei	waṣabiḫo tegabe'
eis ton gunaikōna	bēta anest.
"At dusk she would go	"At dusk she would come
and at dawn she would return	and at dawn she would come
to the harem."	to the harem."

"Now" (two occurrences) (4:14),

en toutǭ tǭ kairǭ.	yom'a.

"Tomorrow" (two occurrences) (5:8),

aurion poiēso to auta.	gēšama egbaro.
"Tomorrow I will do it."	"Tomorrow I will do it."

C. Formulae connected with kingship.

1. The king's ministers: one occurrence (1:14) of

hoi prōtoi parakathēmenoi	ella yenaberu eṭuṭa
tō basilei.	mesla neguš.
"The privy counselors	"The privy counselors
of the king."	of the king."
(lit. "The first sitters	(lit. "Who sat or dwelt apart
next to the king.")	with the king.")

Two occurrences of, e.g. (4:8),

ho deutereuōn tǭ basilei.	za'emtaḫta'a neguš'a.
"The king's prime minister."	"The king's prime minister."
("The second to the king.")	("He who is below the king.")

2. The king's command: one occurrence (2:8) of

kai hote ēkousthē to tou	wasoba
basileōs prostagma.	azzaza neguš.
"And when the king's	"And when
command was heard."	the king commanded."

One occurrence (8:8) of

hosa gar graphetai	esma kwellu zataṣḫefa

tou basileōs epitaksantos.	bate'ezzāza neguš.
"As much as was written at the command of the king."	"Because everything that has been written at the command of the king."

3. The king's will: five occurrences of (3:9),

ei dokei tō basilei.	wa'ema-sa faqada neguš.
"If it seems right to the king."	"If the king wishes."

4. The king's good pleasure: one occurrence (2:17) of

kai ērasthē ho basileus Esthēr.	wa'adamato astēr laneguš.
"The king was pleased with Esther."	"Esther pleased the king."

5. Obedience/disobedience to the king: two occurrences of, e.g. (1:12),

kai ouk eisēkousen autou Astin hē basilissa.	wa'abayat sami 'oto astin negešt.
"And Vashti the queen did not obey him."	"And Vashti the queen refused to obey him."

The use of abaya + infinitive in place of the more obvious isam'a suggests the presence of a formula.

D. Weight formulae: one occurrence (1:7) of

potēria khrusa kai argura... apo talantōn trismuriōn.	waṣewa'at-ni zawarq wazaberur... delew baḫasāba 30,000 maklit.
"Gold and silver cups of thirty thousand talents."	"Golden and silver cups weighing 30,000 talents."

E. Genealogical formulae. One occurrence (2:5) of

kai onoma autǭ Mardokhaios
ho tou Iairou tou Semeiou tou
Kisaiou ek phulēs Beniamin.
"And his name was Mordecai,
son of Yairos son of Semeios
son of Kisaios of the tribe
of Benjamin."

zasemu mardokēwos
walda iya'iru zasemyu
zaqēsyu za'emnagada benyām.
"Whose name was Mordecai
son of Iyairu son of Semyu
son of Qesyu of the tribe
of Benjamin.

The use of walda and za'emnagada appears formulaic.

F. Formulae in reported speech.

1. The command to a messenger, "Say to him," e.g. (4:10-11, 4:8, 4:13),

poreuthēti pros Mardokhaion
kai eipon hote
Ta ethnē panta tēs basileias
ginōskei.
"Go to Mordecai
and say,
'All the nations of the realm
know.'"

ḫor xaba mardokēwos
wabalo
kwellu'a aḫzāb'a lazāti'a
mangešta'a yā'amer'a.
"Go to Mordecai
and say to him,
'All the peoples of this realm
know.'"

kai eipen autǭ
enteilasthai autę̄
eiselthousē
paraitēsasthai ton basilea.
"And she told him
'Tell her
to go
and beseech the king.'"

wayebēlo
balā
teba'
xaba neguš wates'alo.
"And he told him,
'Tell her
to go
beseech the king.'"

Poreutheti kai eipon autę̄
Esthēr, mē eipēs
hoti sōthēsomai.
"Go and say to her,
'Esther, do not say
"I shall be saved."'"

ḫor wabalā
itebali astēr
kama'a aḫayu'a.
"Go and say to her,
'Esther, do not say
"I shall live."'"

2. The verb "to speak" before a quotation, "He spoke saying"; e.g. (4:1, 3:8),

kai ekpedēsas dia tēs plateias eboa phonē̦ megalē̦.	waroṣa enta marxeba hagar enza yeṣarex ba'abiy qāl wayebē.
"And running through the square he cried with a loud voice."	"And he ran through the square of the city while crying with a loud voice, and he said."
kai elalēsen pros ton basilea Artakserksēn legōn.	wanagara la'artakserksēs wayebēlo.
"And he spoke to the king Artaxerxes saying."	"And he spoke to Artaxersxes and he said."

In the first occurrence, yebē is added; in the second it runs counter to the standard translations of the present participle (cf. above, p. 12).

G. Epistolary conventions.

1. The heading: two occurrences of, e.g. (B:1),

basileus megas Artakserksēs.	'abiy arterkserksēs.
"From the great king Artaxerxes."	"From the great artaxerxes."

2. The salutation: one occurrence (E:1) of

khairein.	tefšeḫta lakemu.
"Greetings."	"Greetings to you."

H. Miscellaneous other formulae.

(C:11)

hoti thanatos autōn en ophthalmois autōn.	esma baṣhomu mot gedma a'yentihomu.
"Because their death was before their eyes."	"Because death arrived to them before their eyes."

(C:25)

kurie pantōn gnōsin ekheis.	egzi'o lebba kwellu.
"Lord, you have knowledge of	"God, heart of the universe."

all things."

(5:10)

kai eiselthōn eis ta idia	waḥora bēto
"And going home."	"And he went home."
(6:12)	
Aman de hupestrepsen eis ta idia.	wahama-ni atawa beto.
"But Haman returned home."	"But Haman returned home."
(6:1)	
grammata mnēmosuna tōn hēmerōn.	maṣāḥefta tazkār zanabiyāt zabamawā'ela tekāt.
"The archives." (lit. "The letters, the monuments of the days.")	"The archives." (Lit. "The books of the record of the prophecies which were in the days of old.")
theou di takhous apodontos autǭ krisin	egzi'abḥēr feṭuna fadayo kwennanēhu.
"God quickly passing judgment."	"God quickly passing judgment."
(E:19)	
ekthentes en panti topǭ meta parrēsias.	ṣaḥafkemu bakwellu makān gahāda.
"Posting it in every place publicly."	"Write it in every place publicly."
(E:24)	
hētis kata tauta mē poiēsȩ̄.	za'igabra kamaze.
"Whoever does not do thus."	"Whoever does not do thus."

Some of the foregoing examples obviously make poor tests for formulaic translation. 'elata em'elat may be a formula; but at 3:7 where it translates hēmeran ex hēmerą, it could as easily be a standard mechanical translation. And where the formulaic tendency seems clearer as in 3:9, ei dokei tǭ basilei --> ema-sa fagada neguš, examples would have to be sought over a wider corpus before the phrase could convincingly be shown to be a formula. Syntax, after all, is inescapable; it is there to be studied wherever the language is written; and within even a small corpus, not only is all the syntax theoretically available, much or most of it will actually be employed. Formulae, however, are quite escapable: a given formula may not occur in even a large corpus. Formulae are bound to situations; and for a representative sample of any formula, a wide corpus must be combed for occurrences of its situation.

The designation of the listed expressions as formulae is not, however, entirely arbitrary. Every expression either violates a formal pattern standard elsewhere in the first eight chapters or is part of an institutionalized situation. Most of them are both.

IX. OMISSION, MISTRANSLATION, PARAPHRASE, AND UNPREDICTABLE TRANSLATION.

Of the fifteen hundred ninety three separate syntactic items isolated for analysis in the first eight chapters of the Book of Esther, two hundred sixty nine or 14% do not fit any of the categories in the foregoing analysis. These include mistranslation, paraphrase, omission, and correct but exceptional translation.

Descriptively, the twenty-eight omissions are almost always brief: a word or a phrase, e.g. (2:13, 1:11),

apo tou gunaikōnos heōs tōn basileiōn;	embēta anest . . . . ;
"From the harem to the palace";	"From the harem . . . .;
eisagagein tēn basilissan pros auton.	kama yāmṣe'ewwā lanegešt . . . . .
"To bring the queen to him."	"That they bring the queen . . . . . .

The seventy-five mistranslations are also brief: fairly simple units "cleanly missed" by the translator; e.g. (1:3, A:11),

dokhēn epoiēsen... tois Persōn kai Mēdōn endoksois;	gabra ba'ala... lafars walamēdon walakeburānihomu;
"She gave a party for the nobles of the Persians and Medes";	"She gave a party for Persia and Media and for their nobles";
ho heorakēs to enupion touto kai ti ho theos bebouleutai poiēsai.	ware'ya zanta ḥelma esma egzi'abḥēr fagada yegbar.
"The one who saw this dream and what God was planning to do."	"And he saw this dream because God wished him to.

Of the one-hundred-thirty-three paraphrases, one-hundred-thirteen occur in the translation of the LXX additions to Esther, forty eight in B:1-7 alone. While the language of the rest of the book, as a translation from Hebrew, is to some extent already tamed for Ethiopic, the original language of at least some of these additions is Greek; and its syntax is both very elaborate and completely unsemitic. As a result, misunderstanding, partial understanding, and necessarily radical recasting of language are difficult to keep separate; e.g. (B;2),

eboulēthēn... tous tōn hupotetagmenōn akumatous dia pantos katastēsai bious, tēn te balisleian hēmeron kai poreutēn mekhri peratōn paredsomenos ananeōsasthai, te tēn pothoumenēn tois pasin anthrōpois eirēnēn.	faqadku... astanabireya kwello zalita yetkwēnan za'enbala dengade kama zamogat šari'eya kwello bakama mangšteya šaru'wahedu' watebṣah eska aṣnafa baḫāwert wa'aḫades salāma za'emxaba kwellu sabe' yetfāqar.
"I have wished... to render the lives of (my) subjects completely untroubled and intending to provide a peaceful and completely traversable kingdom, to renew that peace which is desired by all men."	"I have wished... to render everyone who is subject to me without disturbance like a wave (za'enbala - zamogast = akumatous?) and to order everything that my kingdom may be orderly and peaceful and may extend to the ends of the earth. And I will renew peace which is desired by all men.

There are in addition forty-six correct but, from the point of view of our analysis, unpredictable translations; e.g. (2:11, 2:15),

episkopōn ti Esther sumbēsetai;	kama yesma' zenaha la'aster zakama hallawat;

"Checking what was happening to Esther";	"To hear news of how Esther was";
ouden ēthetēsen hōn eneteilato ho eunoukhos.	gabrat kwello bakama azzaza zeku xeṣew.
"She omitted nothing that the eunuch ordered."	"She did everything as this eunuch ordered."

Stated in terms of formal logic, our Chapter One is a particular affirmation,

"These A are B."

In Chapter Two, we will convert and universalize this affirmation to,

"All B are A."

That is, we will convert and universalize the statement,

"These are accurate mechanical translations,"

to the statement,

"All accurate mechanical translations are this,"

which will serve as a hypothesis to be tested in Chapter Three.

Before beginning the conversion, however, we should recall that particular negations, unlike particular affirmations, cannot be converted. Thus the statement,

"These are not accurate mechanical translations,"

yields no statement, however hypothetical, about what accurate translations are. It has no heuristic value. Accordingly, the omissions, mistranslations, and paraphrases described above will have little further part in the thesis, and the figure 269/1593 of 14% unpredictability is almost without significance. We are not attempting to predict -- in fact, no one can -- what does not happen when an accurate mechanical translation is not made but rather what does happen when one is made.

The significant figure is 46/1370 or 3% unpredictability in accurate mechanical translations. This figure represents the empirical residue which may become significant if matched -- on the syntactic level -- by patterns in other Greek-Ethiopic translations.

For the time being, our expectation is that the 3% are gratuitous variations. We expect, in other words, that if the statement

> "These (forty-six) are accurate mechanical translations,"

were converted and universalized to

> "All accurate mechanical translations are this,"

the hypothesis would not be confirmed by further evidence, by which we do not expect that the 3% have no intelligibility but that they not conform to a second pattern of mechanical translation parallel to that of the 97%. Language variations that are gratuitous on one level may be intelligible on another: aesthetics, polemics, psychology, etc. But the only order that concerns us here is that of syntax.

CHAPTER TWO

Translation Decision Charts Derived from the Analysis of Greek-Ethiopic Translation Syntax in Esther 1-8

	Introduction	86
I.	Verb-to-verb subordination	88
	A. Verb + participle	88
	B. Verb + infinitive	91
	C. Verb + conjunction + finite verb	93
II.	Verb-to-substantive subordination	96
	A. Substantive + participle	96
	B. Substantive ± _hōste_ + infinitive	96
	C. Substantive + relative + finite verb	97
III.	Substantive-to-substantive subordination	98
	A. Substantive + genitive substantive	98
	B. Substantive + dative substantive	100
	C. Substantive + preposition + substantive	101
IV.	Substantive-to-verb subordination	102
	A. Active verb + dative object + direct object	102
	B. Active verb + dative object used alone	105
	C. Passive verb + dative abject	107
	D. Verb + adverbial dative	109
	E. Verb + accusative used alone	110
	F. Verb + preposition + substantive	113
	G. Verb + genitive substantive	114
V.	Adjective-to-substantive subordination	115
VI.	Substantive-to-adjective subordination	116
VII.	Coordination of sentences	116
VIII.	Formulaic Language	117

In the hypothesis,

"All accurate mechanical translations are this,"

"this" is the set of Greek constructions dealt with in Chapter One, the set of circumstances that determined them to different Ethiopic constructions, and the set of those Ethiopic constructions themselves. Checking the hypothesis could be no more complicated an operation than reading through the Greek and the Ethiopic of some other translation and seeing whether they matched the expectation set up by Chapter One.

We have preferred, however, to complicate the checking operation slightly by attempting to predict a set of Ethiopic constructions from a set of Greek constructions and then comparing our prediction with the attested Ethiopic text. The device we will use to make the prediction is the decision chart in which various inputs of data about a given Greek construction (Is Y an aorist? etc.) and about the real situation in which it is employed (Is X a person? etc.) flow to different Ethiopic constructions.

The complication serves a purpose in that it begins to make science of what has been uniquely the art of text criticism. It resolves into the repeatable steps of a process that instinct which enables the critic to guess the original behind a translation or the translation that would frow from an original. As arts, version and retroversion sometimes seem simple enough. By dint of familiarity with two languages and with translations from one into the other, the critic knows the shape of the original from the translation and of the translation from the original, and he knows this immediately. But what specific perceptions culminate in his insight? If this question could be answered, then the differing judgments of text critics might be proven wrong or right on evidence. One cannot, after all, argue with another man's art.

Our Chapter One may be regarded as the education of an instinct about the Ethiopic translator of Esther. In moving now from the education to the exercise of that instinct. we want to be careful to exclude any *Sprachgefuehl* not explicitly recorded in Chapter One. The charts serve this purpose. Reading and re-reading Esther 1-8 in Greek and in Ethiopic, we have probably "picked up" more than we know and might predict the Ethiopic of Esther 9 (the first proposed test) better than our charts could. But our purpose here is not to make the best possible prediction of the Ethiopic of Esther 9 but to get the best possible understanding of how such predictions, good or bad are made.

Like a computer, the charts know only what they are told. They do what they are programmed to do and only that. Consequently, when we attempt in Chapter Three to predict the syntax of Esther 9, the history of every prediction will be completely recoverable.

I. VERB-TO-VERB SUBORDINATION.

A. *Greek verb + participle*.

1. Greek aorist predicative participle X + finite verb or infinite Y.

	(a)	(b)	(c)
Is the action of X simply ended before the action of Y begins?	y	n	n
Does the action of X though completed have effects that continue during Y?	n	y	n
Are X and Y simultaneous?	n	n	y
Verb X + verb Y (or verb Y *soba* verb X)	*		
gerund X + verb Y (or verb Y *soba* verb X)		*	
Verb X *enza* imperfect Y			*

2. Greek verb X + present predicative participle Y.

	(a)	(b)	(c)	(d)	(e)	(f)	(g)	(h)
a. Is Y passive?	y	n	n	n	n	n	n	n
Are X and Y cognate?	n	y	n	n	n	n	n	n
Is X *einai*?	n	n	y	n	n	n	n	n
Is the construction: verb of statement X + accusative substantive + accusative present predicative participle?	n	n	n	y	n	n	n	n
Does Y express purpose?	n	n	n	n	y	n	n	n
Does Y express cause?	n	n	n	n	n	y	n	n
Is Y *ekhōn*?	n	n	n	n	n	n	y	
kona + adjective Y	*							
verb XY		*	*					
verb X + *kama* + imperfect Y				*				
verb X + *kama* + subjunctive Y					*			
verb X + *esma* + imperfect Y						*		
verb X + *zabo*							*	
Go to chart I,A,2,b.								*

	(i)	(j)	(k)
b. Is X an imperative?	n	n	y
Is X punctual?	y	n	
Is X durative?	n	y	
verb X + enza + imperfect Y	*		*
imperfect X + imperfect Y		*	

B. Greek verb + infinitive

1. Greek verb of intent X ± *hōste* + dative object + aorist or present infinitive Y.

	(a)	(b)	(c)
Is the subject of Y the subject of X?	y	n	n
Is the subject of Y expressed as the object of X?		y	n
- - - - - - - - - - - - - - - -			
verb X ± *kama* + subjunctive Y, person and number of Y agreeing with X	*		
verb X ± *kama* + subjunctive Y, person and number of Y agreeing with object of X		*	
verb X ± *kama* + subjunctive Y, Y in third plural			*

2. Greek verb of conation or possibility X + infinitive Y.

	(a)	(b)
Is the verb impersonal?	y	n
- - - - - - - - - - - - - - - -		
verb X + *ba*-infinitive Y	*	
verb X + *la*- + infinitive Y		*

3. Greek verb of statement X + infinitive Y -> verb of statement X + kama + indicative Y.

4. Greek verb of action X + accusative + infinitive Y -> causative verb XY.

5. Greek impersonal verb X + infinitive Y -> verb Y.

6. Greek verb X + preposition + infinitive Y.

	(a)	(b)
Is the infinitive aorist or perfect?	y	n
Is the infinitive present?	n	y
verb X + conjunction + perfect Y	*	
verb X + conjunction + imperfect Y		*

C. Greek verb + conjunction + finite verb.

1. Greek verb X + object clause.

	(a)	(b)	(c)	(d)
Is the clause an indirect statement of fact?	y	n	n	n
Is the clause an indirect question of manner?	n	y	n	n
Is the clause an indirect question of quantity?	n	n	y	n
Is the clause an indirect question of fact?	n	n	n	y
verb X + *kama* + indicative Y	*			
verb X + *zakama* + indicative Y		*		
verb X + *kwello za*- or *kwello zakama* + indicative Y (rarely verb X + *zakama* + indicative Y)			*	
verb X + *yogi* + indicative Y				*

2. Greek verb X + adverbial clause.

	(a)	(b)	(c)	(d)	(e)	(f)	(g)	(h)
Does the clause express cause?	y	n	n	n	n	n	n	n
Is the clause a comparison?	n	y	n	n	n	n	n	n
Does the clause express a condition?	n	n	y	n	n	n	n	n
Does the clause express purpose?	n	n	n	y	n	n	n	n
Does the clause indicate time?	n	n	n	n	y	n	n	n
Does the clause indicate the ground of an argument or an action?	n	n	n	n	n	y	n	n
Does the clause indicate a circumstance without indicating its relationship to the main action?	n	n	n	n	n	n	y	n
Does the clause indicate an exception?	n	n	n	n	n	n	n	y
verb X + <u>esma</u> + indicative Y	*							
verb X + <u>bakama</u> + indicative Y		*						
verb X + <u>ema/la'ema</u> + indicative Y			*					
verb X + <u>kama</u>- + subjunctive Y				*				

	(a)	(b)	(c)	(d)	(e)	(f)	(g)	(h)
Does the clause express cause?	y	n	n	n	n	n	n	n
Is the clause a comparison?	n	y	n	n	n	n	n	n
Does the clause express a condition?	n	n	y	n	n	n	n	n
Does the clause express purpose?	n	n	n	y	n	n	n	n
Does the clause indicate time?	n	n	n	n	y	n	n	n
Does the clause indicate the ground of an argument or an action?	n	n	n	n	n	y	n	n
Does the clause indicate a circumstance without indicating its relationship to the main action?	n	n	n	n	n	n	y	n
Does the clause indicate an exception?	n	n	n	n	n	n	n	y
verb X + <u>soba</u> + indicative Y					*			
verb X + <u>nāhu</u> indicative Y						*		
verb X + <u>kama-sa</u> + indicative Y							*	
verb X + <u>enbala</u> + indicative Y								*

II. VERB-TO-SUBSTANTIVE SUBORDINATION.

A. Substantive + participle.

1. Substantive X + active participle Y -> substantive X + za -> active finite verb Y.

2. Substantive X + passive participle Y.

	(a)	(b)	(c)	(d)
Is an Ethiopic getul attested from a root with the meaning Y?	y	y	y	
Is the getul frequently nominalized?	n	y	y	
Is the Agent expressed?	n	n	n	y
Is the Greek participle otherwise verbally modified?		y	n	
substantive X + adjective Y	*		*	
substantive X + za-passive finite verb Y		*		
substantive X + za-active finite verb Y; agent expressed with participle becomes subject of Y				*

B. Substantive X ± hoste + infinitive Y -> substantive X ± kama + subjunctive Y.

C. Substantive + relative + finite verb.

1. Substantive X + hos + finite verb Y.

	(a)	(b)
Is the relative a genitive by attraction; i.e., the equivalent of a genitive demonstrative + accusative relatitive	n	y
substantive X + za-finite verb Y	*	
substantive X + emna za-finite verb Y		*

2. Substantive X + relative adverb + finite verb Y -> substantive X + conjunction + finite verb Y.

III. SUBSTANTIVE-TO-SUBSTANTIVE SUBORDINATION.

A. *Greek substantive + genitive substantive*.

1. Greek substantive X + genitive substantive Y.

	(a)	(b)	(c)	(d)	(e)	(f)	(g)	(h)
a. Is X or Y *therapeia*?	y	n	n	n	n	n	n	n
Is X or Y *aksiōma*?	n	y	n	n	n	n	n	n
Is X used after *eis* or *pros* to express purpose?	n	n	y	n	n	n	n	n
Is X *heis*?	n	n	n	y	n	n	n	n
Is X a proper name?	n	n	n	n	y	n	n	n
Is Y a pronoun?	n	n	n	n	n	y	y	n
Is X preceded by a definite article with demonstrative force?	n	n	n	n	n	n	y	n
verbal transformation	*	*						
kama + subjunctive X + subject/object Y			*					
substantive X + *em*-substantive Y				*				
substantive X + *za*-substantive Y					*			
substantive X-suffix Y						*		
substantive X + *za*-suffix Y							*	
Go to chart III, A, 1,b.								*

		(i)	(j)
b.	Is Y a person?	y	n
	construct substantive X + substantive Y, or substantive X-suffix + la- substantive Y	*	
	construct substantive X + substantive Y		*

2. Greek nominalized article X + genitive substantive Y-> substantive Y in the syntactic position indicated by Greek X.

B. Greek substantive X + dative substantive Y.

	(a)	(b)	(c)
Does Y express possession?	y	y	n
Is Y a person?	y		
Is Y a pronoun?	n	y	
construct substantive X + substantive Y, or substantive X-suffix + *la*-substantive Y	*		
substantive X-suffix Y		*	
substantive X + *la*-substantive Y			*

C. Greek substantive X + preposition + substantive Y.

	(a)	(b)	(c)	(d)	(e)
Is Y an infinitive?	y	n	n	n	n
Is the preposition *kata* used in a distributive sense?	n	y	y	n	n
Is Y preceded by an adjective?		n	y	n	
Is X itself the object of a preposition in a phrase expressing a whole by its extremes?	n	n	n	y	n
substantive X + *kama* + subjunctive Y	*				
substantive X + repeated preposition + substantive Y		*			
substantive X + *za*-substantive Y			*		
substantive X-*ni* *wa*-substantive Y-*ni*				*	
substantive X + preposition + complement Y					*

IV. SUBSTANTIVE-TO-VERB SUBORDINATION.

A. _Greek active verb X + dative object Y + direct object Z_.

		(a)	(b)	(c)	(d)
a.	Is Z _tade_?	y	n	n	n
	Is the Greek _aphairein_, _kakian poiein_, or _kheiras epipherein_?	n	y	n	n
	Is the Greek _perititheinai timēn_, _didonai domata_, or _epibalein kheiras_?	n	n	y	n
	verb X + _la_-substantive Y + _kamaze_	*			
	verb X + preposition + substantive Y + accusative substantive Z		*		
	verb XZ + complement?			*	
	Go to chart IV, A, b.				*

	(e)	(f)	(g)	(h)	(i)
b. Is X <u>poiein</u>, <u>peritithenai</u>, or <u>storennunai</u>	y	y	y	y	n
Is Y a pronoun?	y	y	y	n	
Is Z a pronoun?	n	n	y	y	
Is Z a clause?	y	n	n	n	
verb X + <u>la</u>-suffix Y + clause Z	*				
verb X + <u>la</u>-suffix Y + accusative substantive Z		*			
(verb X-suffix Z + <u>la</u>-suffix Y)			*		
(verb X-suffix Z + <u>la</u>-substantive Y)				*	
Go to chart IV, A, c.					*

	(i)	(j)	(k)	(l)	(m)
c. Is Y a pronoun?	n	n	y	y	y
Is Z a pronoun?	n	n	n	n	y
Is Z a clause?	n	y	n	y	n
verb X + *la*-substantive Y + accusative substantive Z	*				
verb X + *la*-substantive Y + object clause Z		*			
verb X-suffix Y + accusative substantive Z			*		
verb X-suffix Y + object clause Z				*	
verb X-suffix Z + *la*-suffix Y					*

B. Greek active verb X + dative object Y used alone.

	(a)	(b)	(c)	(d)	(e)
a. Is X einai used in the Semitic possession idiom?	y	n	n	n	n
Is X deutereuein?	n	y	n	n	n
Is X khresthai, parakathienai, sumpiein, proserkhesthai, paristanai, epiblepein, homonoun?	n	n	y	n	n
Is X an impersonal verb with infinitive complement?	n	n	n	y	n
ba-complement Y	*				
emtahta-complement Y		*			
verb X + preposition + substantive Y			*		
verb X + nominative Y + kama + subjunctive				*	
Go to chart IV, B,b.					*

	(f)	(g)	(h)
b. Is X *proskunein*, *anaginoskein*, *sēmainein*, *areskein*, *einai*, *boēthein*, *graphein*, *poiein*, *epitassein*, *parakouein*, *aksioun*?	y	y	n
Is Y a pronoun?	y	n	
verb W-suffix Y + *la*-suffix Y, or verb X + *la*-suffix Y	*		
verb X-suffix Y + *la*-suffix Y + *la*-substantive Y, or verb X + *la*-substantive Y.		*	
Go to chart IV, B,c.			*

	(i)	(j)	(k)
c. Is Y a pronoun?	y	n	n
Is Y animate?		y	n
verb X-suffix Y	*		
verb X-suffix + la-substantive Y (less likely: verb X + accusative substantive Y)		*	
verb X + accusative substantive Y (less likely: verb X + *la*-substantive Y)			*

C. *Greek passive verb + dative object*.

1. Greek passive impersonal verb X + dative object Y.

	(a)	(b)
Is the agent of X known?	y	n
active verb X + complement Y, X agrees in person and number with the known agent	*	
active verb X + complement Y, X is in the 3rd person plural		*

2. Greek third person passive imperative X + dative object Y.

	(a)	(b)	(c)	(d)	(e)	(f)	(g)	(h)
Is the subject of X a noun?	n	n	y	y	n	n	y	y
Is X a form of *graphein*, *sēmainein*, etc.?	n	n	n	n	y	y	y	y
Is Y a pronoun?	y	n	n	y	y	n	n	y
active subjunctive X-suffix + *la*-suffix Y	*				*			
active subjunctive X-suffix + *la*-substantive Y		*				*		
active subjunctive X + accusative substantive + *la*-substantive Y			*				*	
active subjunctive X-suffix Y + accusative substantive				*				
active subjunctive X + accusative substantive + *la*-suffix								*

3. Greek passive indicative X + dative object Y.

	(a)	(b)	(c)	(d)
Is Y a pronoun?	y	y	n	n
Does Y indicate the agent?	y	n	y	n
indicative passive X + *emxaba*-suffix Y	*			
indicative passive X-suffix Y		*		
indicative passive X + *emxaba* + substantive Y			*	
indicative passive X + *la*-substantive Y				*

D. *Greek verb X + adverbial dative Y -> verb X + ba-substantive Y*.

E. *Greek verb X + accusative Y alone*.

	(a)	(b)	(c)	(d)	(e)	(f)	(g)	(h)	(i)
a. Is the Greek *balein klērous*?	y	n	n	n	n	n			
Is X *ekhein*?	n	y	n	n	n	n			
Is Y part of an accusative infinitive construction?	n	n	y	n	n	n			
Is X *pimplēnai*, *piein*, *kakopoiein*, *ekpheukesthai*, *phobousthai*, *epikalein*, *adikein*?	n	n	n	y	n	n			
Is Y *theon*?					y	n			
- - - - - - - - - -									
verb XY	*								
nominative Y + *kona* + complement		*	*						
verb X + preposition + substantive Y				*					
verb X + *egzi'abḫēr*					*				
Go to chart IV, E,b.						*			

b.

Is X *aksioun*, *anaginōskein*, *areskein*, *boēthein*, *einai*, *epitassein*, *graphein*, *parakouein*, *poiein*, *proskunein*, *sēmainein*?	y	y	n
Is Y a pronoun?	y	n	
verb X + *la*-suffix Y	*		
verb X + *la*-substantive Y, or verb X + *la*-suffix Y + *la*-suffix Y + *la*-substantive Y.		*	
Go to chart c.			*

	(k)	(l)	(m)	(n)
c. Does Y precede X?	y	n	n	n
Is Y a pronoun?	y	y	n	n
Is Y animate?			y	n
verb X-suffix Y + kiya-suffix Y	*			
verb X-suffix Y		*		
verb X-suffix + la-substantive Y (less likely: verb X + accusative substantive Y)			*	
verb X + accusative Y (less likely: verb X-suffix + la-substantive Y)				*

F. Greek verb + preposition + substantive

1. Greek verb X + preposition + substantive Y

	(a)	(b)	(c)
Is the preposition *eis* or *pros* in an expression of purpose?	y	n	n
Is the preposition *pros* after a verb of speaking, in place of the dative?	n	y	n
verb X + *kama* + subjunctive Y + direct object	*		
verb of speaking X-suffix Y ± *la*-substantive Y		*	
verb X + preposition + substantive Y			*

2. Greek passive verb X + preposition + agent Y.

	(a)	(b)
Is the dative object of X expressed?	y	n
nominative substantive Y + verb X + object	*	
construct substantive X + substantive Y		*

G. *Greek verb X + genitive substantive Y.*

	(a)	(b)	(c)	(d)	(e)
Is X *protobathrein*, *kratein*, *deisthai*, *sterein*?	y	n	n	n	n
Is X *parakouein*?	n	y	n	n	n
Is Y animate ?				y	n
Is Y a pronoun?			y	n	n
verb X + preposition + substantive Y	*				
verb X + *la*-complement Y		*			
verb X-suffix Y			*		
verb X-suffix + *la*-substantive Y (less likely: verb X + accusative substantive Y)				*	
verb X + accusative substantive Y (less likely: verb X-suffix + *la*-substantive Y)					*

V. ADJECTIVE-TO-SUBSTANTIVE SUBORDINATION.

	(a)	(b)	(c)	(d)	(e)
Is there an Ethiopic adjective with the required meaning?	y	n	n	n	n
Is the Greek adjective pronominal?	n	n	y	n	n
Is the Greek pan ethnos or stolē bussinē	y	n	n	n	n
Is Y parthenikos or thaumastos?		n	n	y	n
substantive X + adjective Y	*				
substantive XY		*			
substantive X-suffix Y			*		
substantive X + noun Y in apposition				*	
construct substantive X + noun Y, or substantive X + za-Y					*

VI. SUBSTANTIVE-TO-ADJECTIVE SUBORDINATION.

A. Greek substantive X + adjective Y + complement Z -> substantive X + adjective Y + accusative substantive Z.

B. Greek substantive X + adjective Y + preposition + substantive Z -> substantive X + adjective Y + preposition + substantive Z.

VII. COORDINATION OF SENTENCES.
Greek conjunctions, particles, adverbs -> conjunctions, particles, adverbs;
gar + sentence -> *esma* + clause.

VIII. FORMULAIC LANGUAGE

DATE FORMULAE.

(Charts on following six pages).

	(a)	(b)	(c)	(d)	(e)	(f)	(g)	(h)	(i)	(j)	(k)	(l)	(m)	(n)	(o)
a. Is the date to the first of the month?	y	n	n	n	n	n	n	n	n	n	n	n	n	n	n
Is the date to the day?		y	n	n	n	n	y	y	y	n	n	n	y	y	y
Is it to the month?		n	y	y	y	n	y	y	y	y	y	y	y	y	y
Is it to the year?		n	n	n	n	y	n	n	n	y	y	y	y	y	y
Is the name of the month given?			y	n	y		y	n	y	n	y	y	y	n	y
Is the number of the month given?			n	y	y		n	y	y	y	y	n	n	y	y
Go to Chart VIII, A, b	*														
<u>ba</u>-ordinal + <u>'elat</u>		*													
<u>ba-warexa/awrāxa</u> + month name			*												
<u>ba</u>-ordinal + <u>warex/awrāx</u>				*											

	(a)	(b)	(c)	(d)	(e)	(f)	(g)	(h)	(i)	(j)	(k)	(l)	(m)	(n)	(o)
bawarex/awrāx za-ordinal, zasemu month name or ba-ordinal + warex/awrāx + bawarexa/awrāxa + month name					*										
ba-ordinal ʻām/ʻāmat						*									
ama + day-of-month form + lašarga + warexa/awrāxa + month name							*								
ama + day-of-month form + lašarg + ba-ordinal + warex/awrāx								*							
ama + day-of-month form + lašarg + bawarex/awrāx za-ordinal zasemu month name OR ama + day-of-month form + lašarg + ba-ordinal warex/awrāx + bawarexa awrāxa + month name									*						

	(a)	(b)	(c)	(d)	(e)	(f)	(g)	(h)	(i)	(j)	(k)	(l)	(m)	(n)	(o)
a. Is the date to the first of the month?	y	n	n	n	n	n	n	n	n	n	n	n	n	n	n
Is the date to the day?		y	n	n	n	n	y	y	y	n	n	n	y	y	y
Is it to the month?		n	y	y	y	n	y	y	y	y	y	y	y	y	y
Is it to the year?		n	n	n	n	y	n	n	n	y	y	y	y	y	y
Is the name of the month given?			y	n	y		y	n	y	n	y	y	y	n	y
Is the number of the month given?			n	y	y		n	y	y	y	y	n	n	y	y
<u>ba</u>-ordinal + <u>warex/awrāx</u> + <u>ba</u>-ordinal + <u>'ām/'āmat</u>										*					

	(a)	(b)	(c)	(d)	(e)	(f)	(g)	(h)	(i)	(j)	(k)	(l)	(m)	(n)	(o)
(bawarex/awrāx za-ordinal zasemu month name) OR (ba-ordinal warex/awrāx + bawarexa/awrāxa + month name + ba-ordinal + ‘ām/‘āmat)											*				
bawarexa/awrāxa + month name + ba-ordinal + ‘ām/‘āmat												*			
ba-ordinal + ‘ām/‘āmat + ama + day-of-month form + lašarga + warexa/awrāxa + month name													*		
ba-ordinal + ‘ām/‘āmat + ama + day-of-month form + lašarg + ba-ordinal + warex/awrāx														*	
ba-ordinal + ‘ām/‘āmat + ama + day-of-month form + lašarg + (bawarex/awrāx za-ordinal + zasemu month name) OR ba-ordinal warex/awrāx + bawarexa/awrāxa + month name															*

		(p)	(q)	(r)	(s)	(t)	(u)
b.	Is the date to the year?	n	n	n	y	y	y
	Is the name of the month given?	y	n	y	y	n	y
	Is the number of the month given?	n	y	y	n	y	y
	ama + *ărqa* + *warexa/awrāxa* + month name OR *ama* + *qadāmit* *za*-month name	*					
	ama + *šarq* + *ba*-ordinal *warex/awrāx* OR *ama* + *qadāmit* + *ba*-ordinal *warex/awrāx*		*				
	[*ama* + *šarq* + (*bawarex/awrāx* *za*-ordinal *zasemu* month name) OR (*ba*-ordinal *warex/awrāx* *ba*-*warexa/awrexa* + month name)] OR *ama* + *qadāmit* + (*bawarex/awrāx* *za*-ordinal *zasemu* month name) OR (*ba*-ordinal *warex/awrāx* *ba*-*warexa/awrexa* + month name)]			*			
	ba-ordinal *'ām/'āmat* + (*ama* + *šarqa* + *warexa/awrāxa* + month name) OR (*ama* + *qadāmit* *za*-month name)				*		
	ba-ordinal *'ām/'āmat* + (*ama* + *šarq* + *ba*-ordinal + *warex/awrāx*) OR (*ama* + *qadāmit* + *ba*-ordinal + *warex/awrāx*)					*	

		(p)	(q)	(r)	(s)	(t)	(u)
b.	Is the date to the year?	n	n	n	y	y	y
	Is the name of the month given?	y	n	y	y	n	y
	Is the number of the month given?	n	y	y	n	y	y
	[ba-ordinal ʻām/ʻāmat + (ama + šarq + bawarex/awrāx za-ordinal + zasemu + month name) OR (ama + qadamit + bawarex/awrāx za-ordinal + zasemu + month name)] OR [ba-ordinal ʻām/ʻāmat + (ama + šarq + ba-ordinal warex/awrāx bawarexa/awraxa month name) OR (ama + qadāmit + ba-ordinal warex/awrāx bawarexa/awrāxa month name)]						*

CHAPTER THREE

A Prediction of the Ethiopic Syntax of Esther 9 from the Greek Text

The Ethiopic text of Esther 9 which we shall now attempt to predict is not the text given by E. Pereira in his edition of the work[1] but the text of the ms. which Pereira names Q. For reasons that will be explained, the analysis of our Chapter One was essentially an analysis of Q[2]; and the first attempt to use the charts of Chapter Two for a prediction may reasonably be directed back into Q.

Pereira used four mss. for his edition: n. 55 of the d'Abbadie collection (M), n. 35 of the same collection (N), Add. 24.991 from the British Museum (P), and Orient. 489 from the British Museum (Q). Introducing these mss., Pereira writes (pp. 6-10):

> Manuscrit n. 55 de A.d'Abbadie. ... La copie semble avoir été transcrite, avec soin, d'un livre très ancien; mais elle n'est pas exempte de fautes; il y a des passages corrompus; souvent il manque des lettres, et même des mots....
>
> Manuscrit n. 35. La copie est écrite avec soin et d'après un manuscrit très semblable à celui d'où est transcrite la copie du manuscrit n. 55; mais elle a été révisée par un lettré abyssin, qui a effacé des lettres, des mots et des phrases, et a donné un autre texte. ...
>
> Manuscrit Add. 24. 991 du Musée Britannique. ... La copie semble avoir été transcrite d'un livre très ancien, mais avec peu de soin; il y manque des lettres et même des mots; mais elle a été corrigée par un lettré abyssin, qui a modifié les signes des voyelles, a gratté des lettres et des mots, y en écrit des autres....
>
> Manuscrit Orient. 489 du Musée Britannique. ... La copie semble avoir été transcrite d'un livre très ancien, mais elle a été corrigée, et l'orthographie a été modifiée. ...
>
> Le manuscrit M, du xve ou du xvie siècle, est le plus ancien de tous ceux qui contiennent la version éthiopienne du Livre d'Esther; ce manuscrit contient, non pas assurément la version primitive, mais du moins la version la plus

> ancienne qui soit connue, et sans altération, c'est-à-dire sans les corrections faites dans les siècles postérieurs. Le manuscrit N, de la fin du xviie siècle, contient la même version ancienne que la manuscrit M, mais corrigée; cependant on peut souvent lire encore le texte primitif. Le manuscrit P, du xvii siècle, contient aussi la même version ancienne que la manuscrit M; elle a été corrigée d'après la même exemplaire que la manuscrit N, mais le texte primitif a disparu dans les corrections. Enfin le manuscrit Q, de 1730, contient la version corrigée qui résulte des manuscrits N et P. Le correcteur a fait la révision de l'ancienne version éthiopienne, en la comparant au texte grec des LXX, et il l'a modifiée en tachant de la conformer le plus possible au texte grec; il résulte de là que le texte corrigé constitue une recension du texte ancien.

Pereira's remarks already hint at why Q, though least valuable as a LXX witness, is most appropriate for a study of Ethiopic translation syntax. The Greek text from which Q was made does not have to be reconstructed. It is available in Greek for comparison with its Ethiopic translation. Our attempt to resolve at least a part of the text-critical art into the repeatable steps of a process should obviously begin where both original and translation are available. Thus seventeen times in analyzing Esther 1-8, we abandoned the text offered by Pereira for the readings of Q[3]; e.g. (C:1),

<u>kai edeēthe kuriou</u> <u>mnēmoneuōn panta ta erga</u> <u>kuriou</u>.	(M) <u>wasa'ala</u> <u>enza yezēker kwello zakama</u> <u>gabra egzi'abḥēr</u>.
"And he prayed to the Lord recalling all the works of the Lord."	"And he prayed recalling everything the Lord had done."
	(Q) <u>wasa'ala xaba egzi'abḥēr</u> <u>enza yezēker kwello gebra</u> <u>egzi'abḥēr</u>.

"And he prayed to the Lord
recalling all the work of
the Lord."

Q was preferable at these points simply because the Greek text before us had evidently been its Vorlage.

In another nine lemmata[3], however, Q was preferable for another reason. In these places, it was not superficially any closer to the LXX, but grammatically, it was more consistent with itself and with the usual practice of other mss.; e.g. (3:9),

dogmatisatō apolesai autous. "Let him give the order to have them killed."	(M) ya'azzez wayǝtafe'omu "Let him command and he will kill them";
	(Q) ya'azzez yǝtfe'ewwomu. "Let him command that they kill them."

In our first consideration of the evidence, it became clear that the Ethiopic subjunctive was almost universal as the translation of the Greek aorist infinitive after a verb of intent. M's use of the imperfect at this point was thus exceptional, and this not only by contrast with Q but even by contrast with M in almost every other occurrence of the construction in question. Q then seemed the preferable reading.

It may be objected that a reading which is "preferable" for a syntactic exercise like our Chapter One may not be equally "preferable" for a critical edition. Q does what we want the Ethiopic to do, but what is the gain for the establishment of a LXX witness? Though we are not, just now, concerned with establishing a LXX witness, it may be well to consider the matter further.

Pereira writes (p. 10),

> Pour la version éthiopienne de la Bible, le but de la critique textuelle est, autant que faire

> se peut, de retrouver dans les copies de plus en plus anciennes le texte de la version primitive, aussi exempte d'éléments étrangers que possible. Seul ce texte primitif, c'est-à-dire antérieur aux recensions et révisions qui ont été faites, pur, sans corrections, sans faire attention à sa légibilité ni à son adaptation à un usage quelconque, a de la valeur pour la classification des divers types de texte des LXX et pour la reconstitution de ce texte,

and his position makes sense, but only up to a point; scil., up to the point where he begins to retrovert his text -- "primitif...pur...sans corrections" -- into its original Greek. Only if this further step can be negotiated in a manner subject to some objective control is the LXX text type any closer to reconstitution. In other words, against Pereira's "sans faire attention...à son adaptation à un usage quelconque," we must insist that no Ethiopic ms. is better than any other for purposes of text criticism until attention has been paid to its adaptability to retroversion.

The adaptability of a ms. to retroversion obviously depends on a number of factors. But we would suggest that one of them should be the internal syntactic consistency of the translation language; i.e., the recurrence of given constructions in given situations. Other things equal, the more mechanical the translation syntax, the greater its usefulness for the establishment of a textual witness by retroversion. It is obvious that translation syntax is not always mechanical, but it is just as obvious that only when it is and to the extent that it is can retroversion be effected.

In the absence of the original, the syntax of a given translation ms. can only be established as more or less mechanical by a comparative method. Where, in translations for which the original is available, a given translation construction patterns with a given original construction, that translation construction has an assignable value wherever it occurs. Mss. containing many constructions with such assignable values are then more mechanical than those with few.

It is in this sense that Q is a better ms. than M. Whatever text underlies Q (and at least forty times Q varies from both LXX and M)[4], that text is more perfectly recoverable than M. This is not to say that the Ethiopic constructions of M contain no assignable Greek syntactic values, just to say that Q contains more. Syntactically, Q does more of the time what all the mss. do most of the time. It is in this sense that Q is more mechanical and hence better suited for retroversion.

It may be objected, obviously, that the fact that a given translation construction has patterned with a given original construction in one translation does not give that construction an assignable value in another translation. Our response can only be that if such assignment is impossible, then text criticism is impossible; for this is what text critics do; they assign values to constructions in a translation on the basis of correlations they have observed elsewhere. These correlations may have been observed over a wide variety of texts. They may attain the proportions of the educated instinct we spoke of earlier (p. ...). And yet the methodological problem remains the same.

Many of the foregoing remarks are more germane to Chapter Four, where we shall attempt a retroversion of Esther 10 from Ethiopic to Greek. However, since the prediction of the Ethiopic of Esther 9 is effectively a prediction of Q, we have discussed the use of syntax in text criticism at this point in the study.

And though the retroversion would seem to be of more interest to text criticism, we are beginning with an attempt simply to duplicate the version because, historically, the translation process began this way. The real relationship between these two texts, as that relationship is not constructed but reconstructed, flows from the Greek to the Ethiopic. Retroversion is not a matter of relating the translation to the original, it is a matter of recovering and reversing the relationship which the original once had to the translation. There is a difference.

In the presentation following, the first column gives the Greek text of Esther 9 (Goettingen), the second column gives references to decision-tracks from our Chapter Two, the third column gives the syntax which the tracks predict, and the fourth column gives the Ethiopic Text of Q.

The fraction in parentheses after each verse number is the number of correct predictions over the number of predictions attempted. The blanks inserted at various points in the third column indicate the presence of a word or words about which no more specific prediction is attempted.

The following abbreviations are used: a = addition, m = marginal note, i = interlinear insertion.

9:1 (2/3)

en gar	VII	esma +	esma
tǭ dōdekatǭ	VII,a(i)	ama + day-of-month	(m za) 10 wa 2 awrāx
mēni triskai-dekatę̄ tou		form + lašarq + bawarex/awrāx za-ordinal	ama 10 wa 3
mēnos, hos estin Adar		zasemu month name, or ama + day-of-month form + lašarq + ba-ordinal warex/awrāx + bawarexa/awrāxa + month name +	la'adār
parēn		____ + sub-	bas̄ḥa

ta grammata	II,A,2(d)	stantive + za-	maṣāḥeft
ta graphenta		active verb +	zaṣaḥafa
hupo tou		subject sub-	neguš.
basileōs.		stantive (=	
		agent expressed	
		with participle).	
9:2 (3.5/6)			
en autę tę	IV,F,1(c)	preposition +	wabaye'eti 'elat
hēmerą	V(a)	adjective +	
apōlonto		substantive +	taxāgwelu
hoi antikei	IV,B(j)	verb + verb-	ella qomu
menoi tois		suffix + la-	lā'ela ayhud
Ioudaiois:	VII	substantive	wa'albo
oudeis gar		(less likely: +	
		verb + accusative	
		substantive) +	
		esma + ___ +	
antestē,	I,A,2,a(f)	verb +	zataqatalomu
phoboumenos	IV,E,c(1)	esma + imper-	esma farhewwomu.
autous.		fect-suffix.	
9:3 (3/7)			
hoi gar ar-	VII	esma +	wa-
khontes tōn	III,A,1,	construct	malā'ekta
	b(j)	substantive +	aḥzāb-ni
satrapōn kai		substantive +	wamaqabt-ni
hoi turannoi			
kai hoi basi-	V(e)	___ +	waṣaḥafta-ni
			abayta
likoi gramma-		construct	neguš
		substantive +	
teis		noun, or sub-	

etimon		stantive +	yäkberewwomu
		za-noun, +	
		verb-suffix + la	
		substantive (less	
		likely: verb +	
tous Ioudaious	IV,E,c(m)	accusative	la'ayhud
		substantive) +	
ho gar phobos	VII	esma +	ba'enta ferhata
Mardokhaiou	III,A,1,	construct	mardokēyos
	b(i)	substantive +	
		substantive, or	
		substantive-suffix	
		+ la-substantive +	
enekeito	IV,B,c(i)	verb-suffix.	yetḥazabu.
autois.			

9:4 (4/4)

prosepesen gar	VII	esma + ___ +	esma +
to prostagma		construct	maṣḥafa neguš
tou basileōs	III,A,1,	substantive +	
	b(i)	substantive, or	
		substantive-suffix	
		+ la-substantive	
onomasthēnai	IV,F,1(c)	+ verb +	tasayma
en		preposition +	ba-
pasę̄ tę̄	V(a)	adjective +	kwellu
basileią.		substantive.	mangeštomu.

9:6 (2/3)

kai en	IV,F,1,(c)	preposition +	waba-
Sousois tę̄ polei		substantive +	susā hagar
		___ +	
apekteinan	IV,E,c(m)	verb-suffix	qatalu
		(less likely:	

		+ verb) +	
hoi Ioudaioi		___ +	ayhud
andras		la-substantive (less likely: + accusative sub-stantive) +	
pentakosious.	V(a).	adjective.	570.

9:7 (0/0)

ton te Pharsannestain	wafarasan-hi wanestāyen
kai Delphon	wadalafon
kai Phasga	wafāsgā.

9:8 (0/0)

kai Phardatha	waferdatā
kai Barea	wabaryā
kai Sarbakha	waserabāk.

9:9 (0/0

kai Marmasim	wamarmāsān
kai Arouphaion	wa'arofdeyon
kai Arsaion kai Zabouthaion.	wa'arsēwon wazabotētan.

9:10 (2.5/3)

tou deka huious	IV,E,c(m)	+ la-substan-tive-suffix, or + la-construct substantive (less likely: + accusative sub-stantive-suffix, or + accusative=	daqiqa

		construct sub-	
		stantive) +	
Aman Amadathou	III,A,1,	la-substantive	hāmā weluda
	b(i)	+ substantive,	amadātou
Bougaiou		+ ___ +	buguyāwi
tou ekhthrou	III,A,1,	construct sub-	
tōn Ioudaiōn,	b,(i)	stantive +	ṣalā'ihomu
		substantive, or	la'ayhud
		substantive-	
		suffix + la-	
		substantive	'ašartihomu
kai diērpasan.		+ ___ .	wabarbaru
			baye'eti 'elat.

9:11 (3.5/5)

en autȩ̄	IV,F,1(c)	preposition +	
tȩ̄ hēmerą	V(a)	adjective +	
epedothē te ho	IV,C,3(d)	substantive +	wazēnawewwo
arithmos		passive verb	laneguš
tō̧ basilei		+ la-substan-	xolqwa
		tive +	
tōn apolōlotōn	III,A,1,	construct sub-	sabe' (i zamota)
	b(i)	stantive +	
		substantive, or	
		+ substantive-	
		suffix + la-sub	
en	IV,F,1(c).	stantive, +	ba-
Sousois.		preposition	susā hagar.
		+ substantive.	

9:12 (5/6)

eipen de	IV,F,1(b)	verb-suffix	wayebēlā neguš
ho basileus		+ ___	
pros Esthēr		+ la-substan-	la'astēr

		tive +	
apōlesan	IV,F,1(c)	verb-suffix	qatalu
hoi Ioudaioi		(less likely:	
		+ verb) + ___	
en		+ preposition	ayhud ba-
Sousois		+ substantive	susā
andras	IV,E,c(m)	+ la-substan-	500 wa 70 'edawa
		tive (less likely:	
		+ accusative sub-	
		stantive) +	
pentakosious:	V(a)	adjective;	
en de		proposition +	wa'efo engā
tę perikhōrǫ	IV,F,1(c)	substantive +	ba'adyām
pōs oiei		___ + verb;	gabru.
ekhrēsanto?		accusative sub-	
ti oun	IV,E,c(n)	stantive (less	ment enka
aksiois eti		likely: la-	tāstabaqwe'i
		substantive) +	
kai estai soi.	IV,B,a(a).	verb (less	baqedmēya negri.
		likely: + verb-	
		suffix) + ba-	
		complement.	

9:13 (6/6)

kai eipen Es-	IV,b,c(j)	verb-suffix +	watebēlo astēr
thēr tǫ basi-		la-substantive	laneguš
lei		(less likely:	
		verb + accusative	
dothētō	IV,C,2(b)	substantive) +	habewwomu
tois Ioudaiois		active subjunc-	la'ayhud
		tive-suffix +	
		la-substantive	
khrēsthai	I,B,1(b)	± kama + sub-	kamāhu yegbaru
		junctive (agree-	

		ing with Ioudaiois	
		as subject +	
hōsautōs tēn		___ ± kama +	enta gēšam
aurion hōste		subjunctive-	
tous deka hui-		suffix (agree-	wayešgelu
ous kremasai	I,B,1(b)	ing with Iou-	'ašartihomu
	IV,E,c(m)	daiois as sub-	daqiqa
	V(a)	ject; less like-	
		ly: + subjunctive,	
		etc., but without	
		suffix) + la-sub-	
		stantive-suffix	
		(less likely: +	
		accusative≡con-	
		struct substan-	
Aman.		tive) + adjec-	hamā.
		tive + la-sub-	
	III,A,1,	stantive (less	
	b(i)	likely: + sub-	
		stantive).	
9:14 (5/6)			
kai epetrepsen	I,B,1(c)	verb ± kama +	wa'azzaza
houtōs genes-		3rd plural sub-	kamāhu yegbaru
thai, kai eks-	IV,B,c(j)	junctive + verb-	
ethēken tois	III,A,1,	suffix + la-	wa'azzazomu
Ioudaiois tēs	b(j)	construct sub-	la'ayhud la'ella
poleōs		stantive (less	hallawu westa
		likely: verb	hagar
		+ accusative≡	
		construct sub-	
ta sōmata tōn	I,B,1(b)	stantive +	yešgelu
huiōn Aman	IV,E,c(n)	substantive ±	
kremasai.	III,A,1,	kama + subjunc-	

	b(i)	tive (subject of	
		subjunctive	
		agreeing with	
		tois Ioudaiois;	
		(less likely: +	
		subjunctive-suffix,	
		subject agreeing,	
		etc.) + accu-	šagāhomu
		sative substan-	
		tive-suffix, or	
		accusative sub-	
		stantive≡construct	
		substantive (less	
		likely: + la-sub-	
		stantive-suffix,	
		or la-construct	
		substantive), +	
		la-substantive-	ladaqiqa
		suffix, or la-	
		construct sub-	
		stantive, + la-	
		substantive, or	
		+ substantive.	ḥamā.
9:15 (3/4)			
kai sunēkh-	IV,F,1(c)	verb + ___ +	watagāb'u ayhud
thēsan hoi-		preposition +	westa susā hagar
Ioudaioi en	VIII,a(g)	substantive +	ama
		ama + day-of-	
Sousois tę̄		month form +	10 wa 4 lašarqa adar
tessareskaidekatę̄		lašarqa ± warexa/	
tou Adar		awrāxa + month	
kai apektei-	IV,E,c(m)	name + verb-	waqatalu

nan andras	V(a)	suffix + *la*- substantive +	
triakosious		adjective (less likely: + verb + accusative substantive + adjective) +	*300 'edawa*.
kai ouden diērpasan.	IV,E,c(n)	verb + accusative substantive (less likely: + verb-suffix + *la*-substantive.	
9:16 (3/8)			
hoi de loipoi tōn Ioudaiōn	V(e)	construct substantive + noun, or substantive + *za*-	*wala'ella tarfu ayhud ella yetqanayu*
hoi en tȩ̄ basileia̧ sunēkhthēsan		___ + ___ +	*lanagašt tagāb'u emuntu-hi babaynātihomu*
kai heautois eboēthoun	IV,B,b(g)	verb-suffix + *la*-suffix, or + verb + *la*-suffix, + verb	*watarād'u wa'albo baḥtu zabarbaru*
kai anepausanto apo tōn polemiōn	IV,F,l,(c)	+ preposition + substantive	*wa'a'rafu emna qatlomu*
apōlesan gar	VII	+ *esma* + verb-suffix + *la*-substantive (less likely: + verb +	*wazaqatlu-sa*
autōn murious pentakiskhili-	IV,E,c(m)	accusative substantive) +	

ous tē tris-	V(a)	adjective + ama	ama 10 wa 3
kaidekatē tou	VIII,a(g)	+ day-of-month	lašarqa adār
Adar		form ± lašarqa	10000 wa 100
		± warexa/awrāxa	wa 50
		+ month name +	
		verb +	
kai ouden	IV,E,c(n)	accusative	wa'albo
		substantive	zabarbaru.
dierpasan.		(less likely:	
		+ verb-suffix +	
		la-substantive).	
9:17 (3/5)			
kai anepau-		___ +	eska
santo tē			ama
tessareskai-			10 wa 4
dekatē tou	V(a)	adjective + sub-	
autou mēnos		stantive +	lawe'etu warex
kai ēgon au-	IV,E,c(n)	verb + adjec-	warassayewwā
tēn hēmeran	V(a)	tive + accusa-	laye'eti 'elat
		tive≡substanti-	ba'āla
		ve construct	
		substantive	
		(less likely: +	
		verb-suffix +	
		la-construct sub-	
anapauseōs	III,A,1,	stantive) +	kama bāti
	b(j)	substantive +	yā'refu
meta kharas	IV,F,1(c)	preposition +	mesla tefšeḥt
kai euphro-		substantive.	waṣeqāb.
sunēs.			
9:18 (0/3)			
hoi de Iou-			wa'ayhud-sa

daioi hoi en			ella westa
Sousois tę			susā hagar
polei sunēkh-			tagābe'u
thēsan kai			
tę tessares-	VIII,a(b)	ba-ordinal +	ama 10 wa 4
kaidekatę kai		ʻelat	
ouk anepausanto			wa'iyāʻrafu
ēgon de kai tēn	IV,E,c(n)	verb + accusa-	ye'eta amira
pentekaideka-		tive substan-	wa'ama 10 wa 5
tēn		tive (less	gabru tefšeḥta
		likely: verb-	
meta kharas kai	IV,F,1(c)	suffix + la-	wabaʻāla.
euphrosunēs.		substantive) +	
		preposition +	
		substantive.	

9:19 (9/12)

dia touto oun	IV,F,1(c)	preposition +	wababayna zentu
		substantive +	
		___ + sub-	
hoi Ioudaioi	II,A,2(b)	stantive +	ayhud
hoi diesparmenoi		za-passive verb	ella tazarwu
en pasę khorą	IV,F,1(c)	+ preposition +	westa kwellu
		adjective +	baḥāwert
	V(a)	construct sub-	
tę eksō	V(e)	stantive +	gašf
		noun, or + sub-	
		stantive + za-	
		___, + verb +	
agousin	IV,E,c(n)	accusative	yegaberewwā
tēn tessares-		substantive	šannayta
		(less likely:	laye'eti ʻelat
kaidekatēn		+ verb-suffix	ama 10 wa 4
tou Agar		+ la-substan-	baṣegāb

hēmeran aga-		tive) + ___ +	
thēn met'	IV,F,1(c)	preposition +	
euphrosunēs	I,A,2,b(j)	substantive +	enza yefēnewu
		accusative	
apostellontes	IV,A,c(i)	imperfect +	fetta labiṣomu
		accusative	
meridas hekas-		substantive +	walageromu
tos tǭ plēsion		la-substantive +	
hoi de katoi-	IV,F,1(c)	___; verb +	wala'ella yena-
kountes en		preposition +	beru westa dabra
tais metropo-	IV,E,c(n)	substantive +	ahgur
lesin kai tēn		verb + accusa-	wa'ama
pentekaideka-		tive substan-	10 wa 5
		tive (less like-	
tēn tou Adar		ly: + verb-suf-	yegaberu tef-
hēmeran euphro		fix + la-sub-	šeḥta šannāya
sunēn agathēn	I,A,2,b(j)	stantive) + im-	
		perfect + imper-	
		fect + accusative	
agousin eksa-	IV,A,c(i)	+ la-substan-	enza emuntu
postellontes		tive.	yefēnewu labi-
meridas tois			ṣomu kefla
plēsion.			walageromu.
9:20 (8/8)			
egrapsen de	IV,E,c(n)	verb + accusa-	waṣaḥafo
Mardokhaios		ative substan-	mardokēyos
tous logous		tive (less	lazentu nagar
toutous		likely: verb-	
		suffix + la-	
		substantive) +	
	V(a)	adjective	
eis	IV,F,1(c)	+ preposition	westa maṣḥaf
biblion		+ substantive +	

kai eksapesteilen tois Ioudaiois,	IV,B,c(j)	verb-suffix + la-substantive (less likely: + verb + accusative substantive) + za-	wafannawo la'ayhud
hosoi ēsan en tę̄ Artakserksou basileią tois eggus kai tois makran,	IV,C,1(a) III,A,1, b(i) V(a).	+ verb + preposition + substantive-suffix + la-suffix, or + construct substantive + substantive + la-adjective.	la'ella hallawu westa mangešta artorkorksēs lageburān walarexuqān.

9:21 (2/3)

stēsai tas hēmeras tautas agathas, agein te tēn tessareskaidekatēn kai tēn pentekaidekatēn tou Adar--	I,B,1(b) IV,E,c(n) III,A,1, b(j)	± kama + subjunctive + accusative≡construct substantive (less likely: + subjunctive-suffix + la-construct substantive), subject of subjuntive agreeing with tois Ioudaois, + substantive.	kama yengerewwon (m gba) la'elantu mawā'ela ba'āla ama 10 wa 4 wa'ama 10 wa 5 lašarga adār

9:22 (9.5/14)

en gar tautais tais hēmerais	VII IV,F,1(c)	esma + preposition + adjective + substan-	esma ba'emantu mawā'el

anepausanto hoi	V(a)	tive + verb +	a'rafu ayhud
Ioudaioi apo	IV,F,1(c)	___ + preposi-	emna ḍaromnu wa-
tōn ekthrōn		tion + substan-	ṣalā'ihomu
autōn--kai	III,A,1,	tive-suffix + ac-	
	a(f)	cusative substan-	
ton mēna, en	IV,E,c(n)	tive + za +	bawarex baza
hō estraphē	II,C,1(a)	verb-suffix +	botu gab'u
autois, hos		za + verb + ___ +	
ēn adar, apo	IV,F,1(c)	preposition +	emna lāh
	(four		
	times)	substantive (four	
penthous eis		times) + kama	westa fešḥā wa'-
kharan kai		+ subjunctive	emna ḥēmam westa
apo odunēs eis		+ accusative=	'elat šannāyt
agathēn hēmeran,		construct sub-	zawe'etu adār
		stantive (less	wayegaberewwā
agein holon	I,B,1(b)	likely: sub-	bakwellu mawā-
agathas hēmeras		junctive-suffix	'elihomu kabkāba
gamōn kai eu-	III,A,1,	+ la-substanti-	waṣegāba
phrosunēs eks-	b(j)	ve) + substantive	wayeṣēgewu
apostellontes		+ imperfect + ac-	
meridas tois		cusative substan-	lameskinomu wa-
philois kai		tive + la-sub-	lata'axāhomu.
tois ptōkhois.		stantive.	

9:23 (2/2)

kai prosedeksanto		verb + ___ +	watawakfu ayhud
hoi Ioudaioi	I,C,2(b)	bakama + verb	bakama ṣaḥafa
kathōs egra-	IV,B,b(f).	± suffix	bakama ṣaḥafa
psen autois		+ la-suffix +	lomu
Mardokhaios,		___,	mardokēyos.

9:24 (5/6)

pōs Aman	I,C,1(b)	+ zakama +	zakama

Amadathou ho Makēdōn epolemei autous kathōs etheto psēphisma kai klēron	IV,E,c(1) I,C,1(b) IV,E,c(n)	___ + verb-suffix + zakama + verb + accusative substantive (less likely: verb-suffix + la-substantive)	taqatalomu ḫama walda amadātu za'emna makēdonyā zakama ḫasba wa'astaqāšama
aphanisai autous,	II,B IV,E,c(1).	± kama + subjunctive-suffix.	la'amāsenotomu.
9:25 (7/9)			
kai hōs eiselthen pros ton basilea legōn	I,C,1(b) IV,F,1(c) I,A,2,b(i)	+ zakama + ___ + preposition + substantive + enza + imperfect	wazakama bo'a xaba neguš wasa'ala
kremasai ton Mardokhaion	I,B,1(c) IV,E,c(m)	± kama + third plural subjunctive-suffix + la-substantive (less likely: + subjunctive + accusative substantive)	yesqelo lamardokēyos
hosa de epekheirēsen epaksai epi tous Ioudaious kaka, ep auton egenonto	I,C,1(c) I,B,2(b) IV,F,1(c) IV,F,1(c)	+ kwello za- or kwello zakama + verb ± la- + infinitive + preposition + substantive + preposition + substantive	wakwello zakama xallaya yegbar ekuy lā'ela ayhud gab'a lā'elēhu
kai ekremasthē kai ta tekna autou.	III,A,1, a(f)	+ verb + ___ + substantive-suffix.	watasaqla we'etu wadaqiqu.

9:26 (9/11)

dia touto	IV,F,1(c)	preposition +	wababayna zentu
epeklēthēsan		substantive +	tasamyā
hai hēmerai	V(a)	verb + substan-	emantu mawā'el
		tive + adjecti-	
hautai	IV,F,1(c)	ve + ___ + pre-	dexina zata'aṣa-
Phrourai dia		position + sub-	wa
tous klērous	I,C,2(a)	stantive + esma	esma banagaromu
		+ ba-substantive-	
hoti tę̄ dia-	IV,D III,	suffix + prepo-	yesameyewwon de-
lektǭ autōn	A,1,a(f)	sition + con-	xina ba'enta qā-
kalountai	IV,F,1(c)	struct substan-	la zāti maṣḥaf
Phrourai,	III,A,1,	tive + substan-	
dia tous lo-	b(j) V(a)	tive + adjective	
gous tēs epis-		+ ___ +	
tolēs tautēs			
kai hosa pepon-			
thasin dia	IV,F,1(c)	verb + preposi-	waba'enta kwellu
tauta kai hosa		tion + substan-	zarakabu emnēha
autois egeneto.	IV,B,c(i)	tive + ___ +	wakwellu zakona
		verb-suffix.	lā'elehu.

9:27 (4/6)

kai estēsen,	IV,F,1(c)	___ + verb + ___	wazaṣaḥafu
kai prosedekhon-		+ preposition +	wa'awkafu ayhud
to hoi Ioudai-		substantive +	
oi eph heautois		preposition +	lā'elēhomu
kai epi to sper-		substantive-suffix	
mati autōn kai	III,A,1(f)	+ preposition +	
epi tois pros-		substantive-suf-	
tetheimenois ep	IV,F,1(c)	fix + preposition	
autōn, oude mēn		+ substantive/	kama iyeflesu
allōs khrēson-		verb + prepo-	emzentu gebr

tai. hai de hē-		sition + sub-	wa'elantu mawā-
		stantive + ___.	'el
merai hautai		substantive +	yetgabaru tazkā-
mnēmosunon epi-	V(a)	adjective +	ra eska la'ālama
teloumenon kata	II,A,2(b)	substantive +	'ālam baba'ahgur
genean kai ge-	III,C(b)	za + passive	
		verb + doubled	
an kai polin		preposition +	wabaḫāwert
kai patrian kai		substantive.	wanagad.
khōran.			

9:28 (3/6)

hai de hēmerai	V(a)	construct sub-	wa'elāntu mawā-
hautai tōn	III,A,1,	stantive + ad-	'el yetgabaru
	b(j)	jective + sub-	
Phrourai akhthē-		stantive + verb	zelafu
sontai eis ton	IV,F,1(c)	+ preposition +	esma botu dexnu
hapanta khronon	V(a)	substantive +	kama iyedamsas
kai to mnēmosu-	III,A,	adjective +	tazkāromu la'ā-
non autōn ou mē	1,a(f)	substantive-	lam.
eklipe ek tōn	IV,F,1(c)	suffix + verb +	
geneōn.		preposition +	
		substantive.	

9:29 (3.5/4)

kai egrapsen		___ +	waṣaḫafat astēr
hē basilissa			walata aminādāb
thugatēr Amina-	III,A,1,	construct sub-	wamardokēyos
dab kai Mardo-	b(i)	stantive + sub-	
		stantive, or sub-	
khaios ho Iou-		stantive-suffix	ayhudāwi
daios hosa	I,C,1(c)	+ la-substanti-	kwello zagabru
epoiēsen to	IV,E,c(n)	ve + ___ +	wa'aṣn'ā maṣḫafa
te stereōma		kwello za or	

		kwello zakama +	zamadxānit.
tēs epistolēs	III,A,b(j)	verb + accusative≡	
tōn Phrourai.		construct sub-	
		stantive + construct	
		substantive + sub-	
		stantive.	

9:30 (3/6)

kai mardokhaios			wamardokēyos
kai esthēr			wa'astēr
hē basilissa			negešt
estēsan heau-	IV,B,c(i)	verb-suffix	wa'aḫramewwon
tios kath heau-	IV,F,l(c)	+ preposition +	ware'esomu
tōn kai tote		substantive	
stēsantes		verb (less li-	emnēhu
kata tēs hugi-	IV,F,l(c)	kely: + verb-	wamaḫalu
eias heautōn	III,A,l(f)	suffix) + pre-	baḫeywatomu
kai tēn bou-	IV,E,c(n)	position + sub-	wamekromu.
lēn autōn;	III,A,l(f)	stantive-suffix	
		+ accusative sub-	
		stantive-suffix	
		(less likely: +	
		la-substantive-	
		suffix).	

9:31 (2/3)

kai esthēr			wa'astēr-ni
logō estēsen	IV,D	verb + ba-sub-	baqāla
eis ton aiōna	IV,F,l(c)	stantive + pre-	la'ālam
kai egraphē	IV,F,l(a)	position + sub-	wateṣḥef
eis mnēmosunon.		stantive +	lazekr.
		verb + subjunc-	
		tive + direct	
		object.	

Of the one hundred fifty eight predictions just attempted, one hundred ten and five tenths, or 70%, were correct. However, this figure cannot be matched with the 97% predictability claimed for mechanical translations in Chapter One (pp. 83 ff.). The latter figure, unlike the former, is a predictability in the Ethiopic translation constructions which remain after all those constructions which plainly do not attempt any regularized syntactic patterning with the Greek have been discarded.

Our attempt to predict the syntax of Esther 9 is not, however, primarily a tally. It is an attempt to reduce the selection of translation syntax to a series of binary choices in the thought that the anatomy of the selection, so to call it, might in this way better be understood. Rather than simply collect more data on translations as objects (Chapter One), an attempt is made to describe translation as a process. Since the translator's mind is not available for study, this attempt has to reconstruct the process of translation from the fact (Chapter Two). Finally, in the one hundred fifty eight predictions just attempted, we produce a synthetic "fact" of translation syntax from our reconstructed translation process. By comparing this with the actual translation, we may now hope to refine our ability to reconstruct process from fact; i.e., to modify or increase the number of categories of Chapter One. Unless carried through to such a comparison, even a much higher average in prediction would be of little use. Reviewing the categories of Chapter One then in light of missed predictions of Chapter Three, we note:

I,A,1. No occurrence.

I,A,2. Occurrences at 9:2, 9:19 (twice), and 9:25. 9:19 and 9:25 exactly reverse the aspectual distinction made on p. 13). Perhaps the use of wa- rather than the more common enza- indicates hendiadys. More likely, the syntactic choice within Ethiopic is only weighted either/or; i.e., there is only a lexically determined statistical preponderance of one construction over another for given pairs of verbs. If this is the case, then an adequate decision chart will require not only the durative/punctual aspect of the pair of Greek verbs to be translated but also the position of their meanings on a statistical continuum of Ethiopic meanings. The program obviously becomes extremely detailed.

I,B,1. Occurrences at 9:13 (twice), 9:14 (twice), 9:21, 9:22, and 9:25. Every occurrence except 9:22 matches our expectation. In 9:22, a parenthesis separates the Greek infinitive from the verb of intent, and Ethiopic uses an imperfect in place of the expected subjunctive.

I,B.2. The one occurrence (9:25) is so exactly a verb of conation that the category collapses when the verb does not perform as expected. The class of modal verbs -- if one exists -- would probably be better defined in terms of specific lexical entries like aftana and kehla rather than around a notion like conation. Dillmann's discussion of verb-to-verb subordination (Grammatik, p. 396-406) further suggests that it is only the infinitive without prefixed la- which can be read as modal. The infinitive after la- should be read simply as a less common alternative to (kama +) the subjunctive. After a verb of intent, the translator may thus choose either complement, though his choice is weighted in favor of the subjunctive.

I,B,3. No occurrence.

I,B,4. No occurrence.

I,B,5. No occurrence.

I,B,6. No occurrence.

I,C,1. Occurrences at 9:24, 9:25 (twice), and 9:29 match our expectation.

I,C,2. Occurrences at 9:23 and 9:26 match our expectation.

II,A,1. No occurrence.

II,A,2. Occurrences at 9:1, 9:19, and 9:27. 9:1 and 9:19 match our expectation. In 9:27, the participle, the only verb form in the Greek sentence, is made the predicate in the Ethiopic, Perhaps there is a bias in Ethiopic against the nominal sentence containing a relative clause with a verb. That is, perhaps the sentence wa'elantu mawā'el we'etomu tazakar zayetgabar, etc., would have been unacceptable.

II,B. The one occurrence (9:24) does not match our expectation. Perhaps when the Greek infinitive depends on a noun, the infinitive can be more freely used. But cf. just above, the discussion of I,B,2.

II,C,1. Occurrences at 9:20 and 9:22. Our expectations are matched, but the Greek construction substantive ± preposition + relative + verb should probably be made a distinct category.

II,C,2. No occurrence.

II,A,1. Occurrences at 9:3 (twice), 9:4, 9:10 (twice), 9:11, 9:13, 9:14 (twice), 9:17, 9:20, 9:21, 9:22 (twice), 9:25, 9:26 (twice), 9:27, 9:28 (twice), 9:29, and 9:30. Of these, 9:14, 9:17, 9:21, 9:22 (once), 9:27, 9:28 (once), and 9:29 do not match our expectation. In 9:14, the use of a relative clause "who were in the city" for the genitive "of the city" suggests a parameter of permanence. In 9:17, 9:28, and 9:29, the Greek genitive may be used predicatively; scil., 9:17, "They made that day (a day) of rest"; 9:28, "These days will be celebrated as (the days of) Purim"; 9:29, "She wrote...what she did and the title of the letter was 'Purim'." 9:21 names a day of a month but not by way of giving the date of an action; i.e., not in the dative. For this reason we did not use the date formula. The Ethiopic text of 9:21 suggests, however, that wherever in the Greek a day is named, Ethiopic will tend to translate it as a date. 9:22 seems to be affected by a similar factor. 9:27 is an omission.

III,A,2. No occurrence.

III,B. No occurrence.

III,C. One occurrence at 9:27 matches our expectation.

IV,A. Two occurrences at 9:19 match our expectation.

IV,B. Occurrences at 9:3, 9:12, 9:13, 9:14, 9:16, 9:20, 9:23, and 9:30. 9:3, 9:12, and 9:16 do not match our expectations, 9:3 and 9:12 because the translations are not mechanical, 9:16 because the dative object is a *reflexive* pronoun and no allowance was made in Chapter One for reflexive pronouncs; i.e., for the possibility of translating them by Ethiopic *t*-forms.

IV,C,1. No occurrence.

IV,C,2. One occurrence at 9:13 matches our expectation.

IV,C,3. One occurrence at 9:11 translates the Greek passive by an active third plural in place of the expected *t*-form. It does so for a lexical reason: the *t*-form of the root *znw* is restricted to the reciprocal meaning.

IV,D. Two occurrences at 9:26 and 9:31 match our expectation.

IV,E. Occurrences at 9:2, 9:3, 9:6, 9:10, 9:12 (twice), 9:13, 9:14, 9:15 (twice), 9:16 (twice), 9:17, 9:18, 9:19 (twice), 9:20, 9:21, 9:22, 9:24 (thrice), 9:25, 9:29, and 9:30 match our expectations.

IV,F,1. Occurrences at 9:2, 9:4, 9:6, 9:11 (twice), 9:12 (thrice), 9:15, 9:16, 9:17, 9:18, 9:19 (four times), 9:20 (twice), 9:22 (twice), 9:25 (twice), 9:26 (thrice), 9:27 (twice), 9:28 (twice), 9:30 (twice), and 9:31 (twice) match our expectations.

IV,F,2. No occurrence.

IV,G. No occurrence.

V. Occurrences at 9:2, 9:4 (twice), 9:6, 9:11, 9:12, 9:13, 9:15, 9:16 (twice), 9:17 (twice), 9:19, 9:20, 9:22, 9:26 (twice), 9:27, and 9:28 (twice). 9:6, 9:16 (once), and 9:28 (once) do not match our expectations; 9:16 is an omission; 9:6 and 9:29 may be formulaic.

VI. One occurrence at 9:3 matches our expectation.

VII. Occurrences at 9:1, 9:2, 9:3 (twice), 9:4, 9:16, and

9:22. At 9:2 and 9:3 (once), wa- is used for esma.

VIII. Occurrences at 9:1 (twice), 9:15, 9:16, and 9:18. 9:16 is an omission. Of the others, only 9:15 matches our expectation. The alleged formulae vary so much in detail that one must question whether they should be regarded as formulae at all.

On p. 98, we said that our attempt to predict the Ethiopic syntax of Esther 9 was a check that would accomplish something more than would be accomplished by simply reading the chapter through in Greek and in Ethiopic with our syntactic analysis generally in mind. The prediction has brought to light certain facts that would have been brought to light by such a reading; cf. the comments made about I,A,2; about II,B; about II,C,1; about IV,B; and about VII. However, the prediction has also drawn attention to a syntactic element that would otherwise have been overlooked; namely to word order, to the fact that what happens in the larger unit affects what happens in the smaller.

It is natural enough to imagine that language is built like a house from the bottom up, with no upper story disturbing any lower story; morphemes are built of phonemes, words are built of morphemes, etc. In fact, the higher or larger units do seem often to disturb the lower and concepts like the morphophoneme have to be introduced. Our syntactic analysis in Chapter One dealt with units of only a few words each. The larger units were not considered. However, in Chapter Three as we attempted to predict syntax, the larger units inevitably were considered, for syntax simply does not occur except in sentences.

Working with a scheme based on subordination, we were faced with the anomaly of not being able to include the subject, the main verb, or any other unsubordinated element in our prediction. In view of this and in view of the fact that the decision-tracks took no systematic account of word-order, it is astonishing that word-order was not more of a problem than it was. Our prediction of a verse like 9:20 says much about the underlying similarity of these two apparently so different languages.

However, often enough word-order was a problem, and our inability to predict it affected our control over those smaller elements we had thought to predict. Thus in I,B,1, the intervention of a parenthesis changes the mood of a verb from the expected subjunctive to the imperfect. And thus in II,A,2 and II,A,1, genitive phrases are broken apart in translation by a predicative sense that has to be drawn from the sentence as a whole.

The question, obviously, is how to include word-order in an improved "syntacticon." We would suggest that in the translation of written documents by relatively unsophisticated translators, word-order is dealt with in a distinct step, as the revision of a translation initially made in disregard of any element larger than a phrase. The translator is conscious of words written on a page as soon as he sees them. He becomes conscious of word-order only when his translation makes unacceptably poor sense because a foreign word-order has been introduced into it. As this point, he re-arranges the words of his translation into acceptable order and then, if he is careful, checks his revision against the original.

If this understanding of the "arrival" of word-order in the translation is correct, then word-order would appropriately be introduced into an attempt to automate Greek-Ethiopic translation not as an original component but as a check. This check could take the form of a double series of conditional instructions. A construction drawn from charts like those of Chapter Two would be matched against as complete a list as possible of attested Ethiopic constructions. The construction to be checked would either be on the list or it would not be. If it was, the instruction would be "Use it." If it was not, the instruction would be "Check it."

The instruction "Check it" would be a referral to the

second series of conditional instructions. Here the construction to be checked would be matched against as complete a list as possible of inadmissible constructions likely to result from a mechanical translation of Greek. If the construction was matched by one on the list, the instruction would be a revision. If the construction was not on the list, it would still be only tentatively admissible.

Obviously, the lists described would quickly grow too unwieldy to use as lists. However, just as obviously, the data they contain is not too much for the mind to manipulate as data. Any schoolboy's revision of translation word-order necessarily involves the scanning of an enormous number of discrete items. Practically speaking, he must scan all the allowable constructions in his language -- at least all those he knows -- to reach the negative conclusion that the constructive he has written into his translation is not among them.

The simplest actions, when totally analyzed, are as complex as the splash of a raindrop, and translation is not a simple action to begin with. An analysis of translation -- even the analysis of a single actual translation -- would seem to require the "instant random retrieval" of a great mass of detail, including lexical detail. As both Chapter One and Chapter Three have shown, constructions are not admissible or inadmissible without some reference to lexical items. Effectively, the instruction "Use it" in our first series of conditional instructions is an instruction more like: "Check it word by word. Your construction is admissible for some set of words in the language. Check to see if it is admissible for this set."

The resolution of the translator's art and the critic's recovery of it into science begins to grow so complicated that it would seem impossible to execute it without recourse to computers; i.e., without recourse to a method which eliminates the human element, the instinct, from translation by introducing it in another form.

CHAPTER FOUR

A Prediction of the Greek Syntax of Esther 10 from the Ethiopic Text

Introduction		158
Charts		
I.	Verb-to-verb subordination	160
II.	Verb-to-substantive subordination	163
III.	Substantive-to-substantive subordination	164
IV.	Substantive-to-verb subordination	165
V.	Adjective-to-substantive subordination	168
VI.	Substantive-to-adjective subordination	168
VII.	Coordination of sentences	168
VIII.	Formulaic language	168
Text		169

In an attempt to predict Greek syntax from its Ethiopic translation, we will now reverse the charts of our Chapter Two and, from that reversal, predict as much of the syntax of Esther 10 as we can.

The reversal is accomplished simply by listing the Ethiopic constructions which occur in the lower half of the charts of Chapter Two with a reference to where in the chapter each occurs. The main headings -- verb-to-verb, verb-to-substantive, substantive-to-substantive, substantive-to-verb, adjective-to-substantive and substantive-to-adjective -- are retained.

It will immediately be noted that after some of the reversed entries, two or more references are given. The selection of one reference -- i.e., of one construction -- over the others is made in at least three ways.

Sometimes the selection can be made by using the extra-linguistic information on the charts. Thus after III, 2, "Substantive X + za-substantive Y," three references are given: III, A,l,a(e); III,C(c); and V(e). In the track leading to III,A,l(e), however, we find the question, "Is X a proper name?"; and in the track leading to III,C(c), we find the question, "Is the preposition kata used in a distributive sense?" which includes a question about whether the phrase is distributive at all. Since these questions can be answered by reference to the Ethiopic alone, the choice of the remaining reference, V(e), is fairly automatic. Cf. below F:II.

In many other cases, the charts can be used in choosing one construction over another, but not in so automatic a fashion. Thus after IV, 15, "Verb X + preposition + substantive Y," the first entry tracks back through the question "Is X khrēsthai, parakathienai, sumpiein, proserkhesthai, paristanai, epiblepein, or homonoun?" Strictly speaking, the question cannot be answered from the Ethiopic alone; but one can guess, in a given case, that translation by any of these verbs would be most unlikely.

On a few occasions, the choice of one reference over the others is made on the basis of information not on the charts at all. Thus at IV, 20, "Verb X-suffix + la-substantive Y," there are five possible references. In predicting F:9, we choose the fifth reference, IV, G (d), verb X + genitive substantive Y, because the Ethiopic verb tazakkara suggests the Greek mnemoneuein, which takes a genitive object.

The higher percentage of correct predictions -- 79/90 or 88% -- in our syntactic retroversion of Esther 10 is thus partly due to a different definition of correctness and partly due to employment on a few occasions of unprogrammed information. It may also be due to the fact that the Greek of Esther 10 is clear in meaning and fairly simple, while the Greek of Esther 9 is on occasion almost incomprehensible (cf. the still higher percentages in Chapter Five).

I. VERB-TO-VERB SUBORDINATION.

1. Verb X + verb Y.

Are X and Y both imperfects?	y	n
A,2,b(j)	*	
I,A,1(a)		*

2. Gerund X + verb Y. I,A,1(b).

3. Verb Y *soba* verb X. I,A,1(b) or I,C,2(e).

4. Verb Y *emdexra* verb X. I,A,1(a).

5. *kona* + adjective Y. I,A,2,a(a).

6. Verb X + conjunction + imperfect Y.

Is the conjunction *kama*?	y	y	n
Is X a verb of statement?	y	n	
Is the conjunction *enza*?	n	n	y
I,A,2,a(d) or I,B,6,(b) or I,C,1(a) or I,B,3	*		
I,B,6(b)		*	
I,A,1(c) or I,A,2,b(i or k) or I,B,6(b)			*

7. Verb X + conjunction + perfect. I,B,6(a).

8. Verb X ± *kama* + subjunctive Y.

Is X a verb of intent?	y	y	n	
Do the person and number of Y agree with X?	y	n	n	
Do the person and number of Y agree with the object of X?	n	y	n	
Is Y a third plural, no object expressed after X?	n	n	y	
I,B,1(a)	*			
I,B,1(b)		*		
I,B,1(c)			*	
I,A,2,a(e) or I,C,2(d) or III,A,1, a(c) or IV,F,1(a) or IV,B,a(d)				*

9. Verb X + *zakama* + indicative Y. I,C,1(b).

10. Verb X + *kwello za-* or *kwello zakama* + indicative Y. I,C,1(c).

11. Verb X + *yogi* + indicative Y. I,C,1(d) or I,B,6 (a,b).

12. Verb X + *esma* + indicative Y. I,C,2(a); or if Y is imperfect, I,A,2,a(f); or VII; or I,B,6(a,b).

13. Verb X + *bakama* + indicative Y. I,C,2(c) or I,B,6(a,b)

14.	Verb X + ema/la'ema + indicative Y.	I,C,2(c) or E,B,6(a,b)
15.	Verb X + nāhu + indicative Y.	I,C,(f) or I,B,6(a,b)
16.	Verb X + kama-sa + indicative Y.	I,C,2(g) or I,B,6(a,b)
17.	Verb X + enbala + indicative Y.	I,C,2(h) or I,B,6(a,b)
18.	Verb X + ba-infinitive Y.	I,B,2(b).
19.	Verb X + la-infinitive Y.	I,B,2(b).
20.	Verb X + zabo.	I,A,2,a(g).
21.	Causative verb.	I,B,4.

II. VERB-TO-SUBSTANTIVE SUBORDINATION.

1. Substantive X + za-active verb Y.	II,A,1 or II,A,2 or II,C,1(a) or V(e)
2. Substantive X + adjective Y.	II,A,2(a,c) or V(a).
3. Substantive X + za-passive finite verb Y.	II,A,2(b).
4. Substantive X ± kama + subjunctive Y.	II,B.
5. Substantive X + emna za-finite verb Y.	II,C,1(b)
6. Substantive X + conjunction + finite verb Y.	II,C,2.

III. SUBSTANTIVE-TO-SUBSTANTIVE SUBORDINATION.

1.	Substantive X + em-substantive Y.	III,A,1,a(d).
2.	Substantive X + za-substantive Y.	III,A,1,a(e) III,C(c) or V(e).
3.	Substantive X-suffix Y.	III,A,1,a(f) or III,B(b) or V(c).
4.	Substantive X + za-suffix Y.	III,A,1,a(g).
5.	Construct substantive X + substantive Y.	III,A,1,b(i or J) or III,B(a) or IV,F,2(b) or V(e).
6.	Substantive X-suffix + la- substantive Y.	III,A,1,b(i) or III,B(a).
7.	Substantive X + la-substantive.	III,B(c).
8.	Substantive X + kama + subjunctive Y.	III,C (a).
9.	Substantive X + repeated preposition-substantive Y.	III,C(b).
10.	Substantive X-ni + wa-substantive Y-ni.	III,C,(d)
11.	Substantive X + preposition + complement Y.	III,C(e)

IV. SUBSTANTIVE-TO-VERB SUBORDINATION.

1.	Verb X + la-substantive Y + kamaze.	IV,A,a(a)
2.	Verb X + preposition + substantive Y + accusative substantive Z.	IV,A,a(b)
3.	Verb XZ (akbara, faṭaṭa, qaṭala) + complement Y.	IV,A,a(c)
4.	Verb X + la-suffix Y + clause Z.	IV,A,b(e)
5.	Verb X + la-suffix Y + accusative substantive Z.	IV,A,b(f)
6.	Verb X-suffix Z + la-suffix Y.	IV,A,b(g)
7.	Verb X-suffix Z + la-substantive Y.	IV,A,c(h)
8.	Verb X + la-substantive Y + accusative substantive Z.	IV,A,c(i)
9.	Verb X + la-substantive Y + object clause Z.	IV,A,c(j)
10.	Verb X-suffix Y + accusative substantive Z.	IV,A,c(k)
11.	Verb X-suffix Y + object clause Z.	IV,A,c(l)
12.	Verb X-suffix Z + la-suffix Y.	IV,A,c(m)
13.	ba-complement Y in possession idiom.	IV,B,a(a)

14.	_emtaḥta_-complement Y in sense of "second in charge."	IV,B,a(b)
15.	Verb X + preposition + substantive Y.	IV,B,a(c) or IV,F,1(c) IV,E,a(d) or IV,G(a).
16.	Verb X + _la_-suffix Y.	IV,B,b(f) or IV,E,b(g)
17.	Verb X + _la_-suffix Y + _la_-substantive Y.	IV,E,b(h)
18.	Verb X-suffix Y + _la_-suffix Y + _la_-substantive Y.	IV,B,b(g)
19.	Verb X + _la_-substantive Y.	IV,B,b(g) or IV,E,b(h) or IV,G(b)
20.	Verb X-suffix + _la_-substantive Y.	IV,B,b(f) or IV,B,c(j, less likely k) or IV,E,c(m, less likely n) or IV,G(d, less likely e).
21.	Verb X + accusative substantive Y.	IV,B,c (k, less likely j) or IV,E,c(n, less likely m) or IV,G (e, less likely d).
22.	Verb X-suffix Y.	IV,B,c(i) or IV,E,c(l) or IV,G(c) or IV,E,a(b)
23.	Verb X-suffix Y + _kiya_-suffix Y.	IV,E,c(k)
24.	Verb of speaking X-suffix Y.	IV,F,1(b)

25.	Verb of speaking X-suffix Y + la-substantive Y.	IV,F,1(b)
26.	Active verb X + complement Y, X in 3rd person plural impersonal.	IV,C,1(b)
27.	Active subjunctive X-suffix + la-substantive Y.	IV,C,2(b)
28.	Active subjunctive X-suffix + la-suffix Y.	IV,C,2(a)
29.	Active subjunctive X + accusative substantive + la-substantive Y.	IV,C,2(c)
30.	Active subjunctive X-suffix Y + accusative substantive.	IV,C,2(d)
31.	Active subjunctive X + accusative substantive + la-suffix Y.	IV,C,2(h)
32.	Passive verb X + emxaba-suffix Y.	IV,C,3(a)
33.	Passive verb X-suffix Y.	IV,C,3(b)
34.	Passive verb X + emxaba + substantive Y.	IV,C,3(c)
35.	Passive verb X + la-substantive Y.	IV,C,3(d)
36.	Verb X + ba-substantive Y.	IV,D or IV,F,1(c)
37.	asta'aṣawa.	IV,E,a(a)
38.	Verb X + egzi'abḥēr.	IV,E,a(e)

V. ADJECTIVE-TO-SUBSTANTIVE SUBORDINATION.

1. Substantive X + adjective Y. V(a).

2. Substantive X + noun Y in apposition. V(d)

VI. SUBSTANTIVE-TO-ADJECTIVE SUBORDINATION.

1. Substantive X + adjective Y + accusative substantive Z. VI,A.

2. Substantive X + adjective Y + preposition + substantive Z. VI,B.

VII. COORDINATION OF SENTENCES.

1. _esma_ + clause. VII.

VIII. FORMULAIC LANGUAGE: NO PREDICTION POSSIBLE.

Note: in the section that follows, the fraction in parentheses immediately following each verse number gives the number of correct predictions over the number of predictions attempted.

The letter _m_ indicates a marginal addition.

In each entry, the Ethiopic text is at the upper left; the reference numbers from the reversal chart as just given are at the upper right; the syntax predicted is at the lower left; and the Greek text is at the lower right.

Esther 10:1 (1/2)

waṣaḥafa neguš	IV,15
westa mangeštu	III,3.
zabamedr wazababeḥēr.	

Verb + ___ +	egrapsen de ho basileus
preposition + substantive +	epi tēn basileian
genitive pronoun + ___ .	tēs te gēs kai tēs thalassēs.

10:2 (8/11)

walā'ela ṣan'u	IV, 15; III,3
waqatalewwomu	IV,22
walā'ela be'lu	IV,15; III,3
wakebra mangeštu	III,5; III,3
nāhu leku'	II,2
westa maṣḥafa fars wazamēdon	VI,2; III,5
latazkār.	VI,2.

Preposition + substantive + genitive pronoun +	kai tēn iskhun autou
verb + accusative pronoun +	kai andragathian,
preposition + substantive + genitive pronoun +	plouton
substantive + genitive substantive + genitive pronoun +	te kai doksan tēs basileias autou: idou
___ + adjective + preposition + substantive + genitive	gegraptai en bibliǭ basileōn Persōn kai Medōn
substantive + ___ + preposition + substantive.	eis mnēmosunon.

10:3 (6/10)

mardokēyos bāḫtitu	V,1
yā'aqeb mangešta neguš	IV,21
artorkorksēs.	III,5
'abiy we'etu mangeštu wakebur	V,1; III,3; V,1; VI,2
baxaba ayhud	
wayetfāqar wayenager	I,1
nebratā lakwellu ḫezba.	IV,8; V,1.

Substantive + adjective +	ho de Mardokhaios
verb + accusative substantive	diedekheto ton basilea
+ genitive substantive + ___ .	Artakserksēn
Adjective + ___ + substantive	kai megas en tē̦ basileią kai
+ genitive substantive + ad-	dedoksamenos
jective + preposition + sub-	hupo tōn Ioudaiōn
stantive + present participle	kai philoumenos
+ present or imperfect +	diegeito
accusative substantive + da-	tēn agōgēn panti tō̦ ethnei
tive substantive.	autou.

F:1 (1.5/2)

wayebē mardokēyos	
emxaba egzi'abḫēr	IV,15
kona zentu nagar.	V,1

___ +	Kai eipen Mardokhaios
preposition + substantive +	Para tou theou
verb + adjective + substan-	egeneto tauta:
tive.	

F:2 (6/7)

tazakkarku ba'enta ḥelm	IV,15
zare'iku babayna zentu nagar	II,1; IV,15; V,1
esma ixalafa	VII
emnēhu lawe'etu ḥelm	IV,15; V,1.
qāla.	

Verb + preposition + substan-	*emnēsthēn gar peri tou enupniou*
tive + *hos* + verb + preposi-	*hou eidon peri tōn logōn*
tion + adjective + substantive	*toutōn: oude gar parēlthon*
+ verb + *gar* + preposition +	*ap autōn*
adjective + substantive.	*logos.*

F:3 (9/12)

entākti nestit naq'a māy	V,1; V,1; III,5
enta konat falga	II,1
wakona berhāna ḍaḥay	II,1; III,5
wamāy bezux.	V,1
astēr ye'eti falg	V,1
enta awsabā neguš	II,1; IV,22
warassayā negešta.	IV,22; IV,21.

Adjective + adjective + sub-	*hē mikra pēgē,*
stantive + genitive substan-	*hē egeneto potamos*
tive + *hos* + verb + ___ +	*kai ēn*
verb + substantive + genitive	*phōs kai hēlios*
substantive + substantive	*kai hudōr polu:*
+ adjective.	
___ + adjective + substan-	*Esthēr estin ho potamos,*
tive + *hos* + verb + accusa-	*hēn egamēsen ho basileus*
tive pronoun + ___ +	
verb + accusative pronoun +	*kai epoiēsen basilissan.*
accusative substantive.	

F:4-5 (5/5)

wa'elketu kel'ētu kayesi	V,1; V,1
ana waḫamā neḫna.	
wa'aḫzāb-sa	
ella tagābe'u kama	II,3
yāmāsenu semomu la'ayhud	I,8; III,6

Adjective + adjective +	hoi de duo drakontes
substantive + ___ .	egō eimi kai Aman.
___ + passive participle	ta de ethnē ta episunakhthenta
± hōste + infinitive +	apolesai to onoma
accusative substantive +	
genitive substantive.	tōn Ioudaiōn.

F:6 (13/13)

waḥezb zazi'aya	III,4
esrā'el	
we'etu ella ya'āwayewwu	II,1
xaba egzi'abḥēr	IV,15
wadexnu	
wa'adxānomu egzi'abḥēr	IV,20
laḥezbu	III,3
wa'adxānana egzi'abḥēr	IV,22
emna zentu kwellu ekuy.	IV, 15; V,1; V,1
wagabra egzi'abḥēr ta'āmera	IV,21
wamadmema 'ābayta	V,1
za'ikona kamāhu westa aḥzāb.	II,1; IV,15.

Article with demonstrative force + substantive + article + genitive pronoun + substantive + ___ + hos + verb + preposition + substantive + verb + verb + ___ + + accusative substantive + genitive pronoun + verb + accusative pronoun + ___ + preposition + adjective + adjective + substantive. verb + ___ + accusative substantive + accusative substantive + adjective + hos + verb + ___ + preposition + substantive.	to de ethnos to emon houtos estin Israēl, hoi boēsantes pros ton theon kai sōthentes: kai esōsen kurios ton laon autou, kai erusseto kurios hēmas ek pantōn tōn kakōn toutōn, kai epoiēsen ho theos ta sēmeia kai ta terata ta megala, ha ou gegonen en tois ethnesin.

F:7 (7/7)

wababayna zentu	IV,15
gabra kel'ēta kefla	IV,21; V,1
aḫada laḫezba egzi'abḫēr	IV,8; III,5
wa'aḫada lakāle' ḫezb.	IV,8; V,1.

Preposition + substantive +	dia touto
verb + adjective + accusative	epoiēsen klērous duo,
substantive + accusative sub-	hena
stantive + dative substantive	tō̧ laō̧
+ genitive substantive + ac-	tou theou
cusative substantive + dative	kai hena
substantive + adjective.	pasin tois ethnesin.

F:8 (7/8)

wabaṣḫa 1 (m 2) kefl	V,1
basa'at wabagizē	IV,15; IV,15
waba'elata dayn	IV,15; III,5
qedma egzi'abḫēr	IV,15
walā'ela kwellu aḫzāb.	IV,15; V,1

Verb + substantive +	kai ēlthon hoi duo klēroi
adjective + preposition +	houtoi eis hōran kai
substantive + preposition +	kairon kai eis
substantive + preposition +	
substantive + genitive sub-	hēmeran kriseōs
stantive + preposition +	enōpion tou theou
substantive + preposition +	kai pasin tois ethnesin.
adjective + substantive.	

F:9 (4/4)

watazakkaromu egzi'abḫēr	IV,20
laḫezbu	III,3
wa'anṣeḫa resto.	IV,21; III,3
Verb + ___ + genitive substantive + genitive pronoun + verb + accusative substantive + genitive pronoun.	*kai emnēsthē ho theos tou laou autou kai edikaiōsen tēn klēronomian heautou.*

F:10 (6/10)

wakona la'elāntu mawā'el	IV,15; V,1
warexa adār	
ama 10 wa 4 wa'ama 10 wa 5	
lašarqa we'etu warex	
enza yetgābe'u	I,6
batefšeḫt	IV,15
qedma egzi'abḫēr	IV,15
batewledomu	IV,15; III,3
la'ālam	IV,15
westa esrā'el ḫezbu.	IV,15; III,3.
Verb + preposition + substantive + adjective + ___ +	*kai esontai autois hai hēmerai hautai en mēni Adar tēͅ tessareskaidekatēͅ kai tēͅ pentekaidekatēͅ tou autou*
participle + preposition + substantive + preposition + substantive + preposition + substantive + genitive pronoun + preposition + substantive + preposition + substantive + substantive + suffix.	*mēnos meta sunagōgēs kai kharas kai euphrosunēs enōpion tou theou kata geneas eis ton aiōna en tōͅ laōͅ autou Israēl.*

F:11 (4/9)

ama rābeʻt ʻāmata mangeštu	
lapatalomēwos wagalēyopētra	
abdos egziʼabḫēr zayebē	II,1
re'us kāhen walēwāwi	V,1
wapatolomāwi waldu	III,3
wayetwēkaf maṣḥafa	IV,21
enta bāti dexin	II,1
enta yebēlo hallawat	II,1; IV,22
watargwamā	III,3
lasimakos patolomāwi	III,7
za'iyarusālēm.	III,2

___ +	*Etous tetartou basileuontos*
	Ptolemaiou kai Kleopatras
substantive + *hos* + verb +	*eisēnegken Dositheos*
adjective + substantive +	*hos ephē einai hiereus kai*
___ + substantive +	*Leuitēs, kai Ptolemaios*
genitive pronoun + verb +	*ho huios autou*
accusative substantive +	*tēn prokeimenēn epistolēn*
hos + verb + dative pronoun +	*tōn Phrourai*
___ + substantive + genitive	*hēn ephasan einai,*
pronoun + dative pronoun +	*kai hermēneukenai Lusimakhon*
___ + adjective.	*Ptolemaiou, tōn en Ierousalēm*.

CHAPTER FIVE

A Prediction of the Ethiopic Syntax of III 'ezrā 3 from the Greek Text and a Prediction of the Greek Syntax of IV Baruch from the Ethiopic Text

Introduction 178
1 Esdras (III 'ezrā) 178
IV Baruch 192
Conclusion 199

As suggested above, syntax can only be automatically predicted when the order of words in larger units has been programmed into the "syntacticon" in the form of a check. However, even in dealing with the smaller units, it may well be asked whether an analysis based only on the Book of Esther will hold true for other works. Can the Ethiopic syntax of other works be predicted from the Greek or the Greek from the Ethiopic using an analysis based only on Esther? We should at the very least expect corrections and refinements to come with each expansion of the corpus, but perhaps the analysis of our Chapters One and Two cannot be taken even as *point de départ*.

This is the question we have in mind as, in the present chapter, we attempt, first, to predict the Ethiopic syntax of III ʻezra 3 from the Greek of 1 Esdras 3 and, second, to predict the Greek syntax of IV Baruch 1 from the Ethiopic text of the same work.

1 Esdras 3:1 (5/7)

kai ephthasen	
ho mēn ho hebdomos	V(a)
kai hoi huioi israēl	III,A,1,b(j)
en polesin autōn	III,C(e); III,A,1,a(f)
kai sunēkhthē ho laos	
hōs anēr heis	III,C(e); V(a)
eis hierousalēm.	IV,F,1(c).

___ +	*wabaṣḫa*
substantive + adjective +	*sābeʻ warex*
construct substantive + sub-	*wa'esrā'ēl*
stantive + preposition + sub-	*westa ahgurihomu hallawu*
stantive + genitive substantive	
+ verb + substantive + prepo-	*wa'emza tagābe'u ḫezb*
sition + substantive + ad-	*westa iyarusālēm xebura*
jective + preposition +	*kama aḫadu be'esi.*
substantive.	

3:2 (10.5/11)

kai anestē iēsous	
ho tou iōsedek	formula?
kai hoi adelphoi autou	III,A,1,a(f)
hoi hiereis, kai	
zorobabel ho tou salathiēl,	formula?
kai hoi adelphoi autou	III,A,1,a(f)
kai ǭkodomēsan to thusiastē-	IV,E,c(n)
rion tou theou israēl	III,A,1,b(i)
tou anenegkai ep autǭ	III,A,1,b(j)
holokautōseis,	I,B,1(a); IV,F,1(c)
kathōs gegraptai	I,C,2(b)
en nomǭ mōusē	IV,F,1(c); III,A,1,b(j)
anthrōpou tou theou.	III,A,1,b(i).

___ + substantive-suffix +	watanše'a iyosēs walda iyosēdēq
___ +	wa'axāwiha kāhnāt wazarubābēl
___ + substantive-suffix +	walda salātyāl wa'axāwihu
verb + accusative=construct substantive, or accusative substantive-suffix (less likely: verb-suffix + la-construct substantive [or + la-substantive-suffix]) + substantive (or + la-substantive) ± kama + 3rd plural subjunctive + accusative (less likely: 3rd plural subjunctive-suffix + la-substantive) + preposition + substantive +	waḫanaṣu mešwā'ā amlāka esrā'ēl kama yegbaru mašwā'ta westētu
bakama + verb + preposition + construct substantive + substantive, or + substantive-suffix + la-substantive, +	bakama ṣeḫuf westa orita mosē
substantive-suffix + la-substantive, or + construct substantive + substantive.	be'esē egzi'abḫēr.

3:3 (8/10)

Kai hētoimasan to thusiastē-	IV,E,c(n)
rion epi tēn hetoimasian au-	IV,F,l(c); III,A,l,a(f)
tou, hoti en katapleksei	I,C,2(a); IV,F,l(c)
ep autous	IV,F,l(c)
apo ton laōn tōn gaiōn.	III,C(e); III,A,l,b(j)
kai anebibasan ep autǭ	IV,A,c(i); IV,F,l(c)
holokautōseis tǭ kuriǭ	
to prōi kai eis hesperan.	formula?

Verb + accusative substantive	*waḫanaṣewwo lamešwa‘*
(less likely: verb-suffix +	*bakama šer‘atu*
la-substantive) + preposition	
+ substantive + genitive	
substantive + *esma* +	*esma ferhat*
preposition + substantive +	*lā‘elēhomu*
preposition + substantive +	*emna aḫzāba medr*
preposition + construct sub-	
stantive + substantive.	
Verb + accusative substantive	*wa'a‘ragu mašwā‘ta westētu*
+ *la*-substantive + preposition	*la'egzi'abḫēr*
+ substantive + ___.	*zanageh-ni wazasark-ni.*

3:4 (4/5)

kai epoiēsen	IV,E,c,(n)
tēn heortēn tōn skeuōn	III,A,1,b(j)
kata to gegrammenon,	IV,F,1(c)
kai holokautōseis	IV,E,c(n)
hēmeran en hēmerą en arithmǭ	formula?
hōs hē krisis,	I,C,2(b)
logon hēmeras in tę̄ hēmerą autou.	formula?

Verb + accusative=construct substantive, or + accusative substantive-suffix (less likely: verb-suffix + la-construct substantive, or la-substantive-suffix), + substantive, or + la-substantive,	wagabru ba'āla maṣalat
+ preposition + substantive	zakama ṣeḥuf
+ accusative substantive (less likely: + la-substantive)	wamaśwā'et-ni
+ ___ + bakama + substantive + ___ .	zababa'elat xwelqwa bakama śer'āta ḥezb mawā'elihu lala'elatu.

3:5 (5/10)

kai meta touto	IV,F,1(c)
tēn holokautōsin	IV,E,c(n); III,A,1,b(j)
tou endelekhismou	
kai eis tas noumēnias,	IV,F,1(c)
kai eis tas heortas	IV,F,1(c)
tǭ kuriǭ	
tas hēgiasmenas	II,A,2(b); IV,C,3(d)
kai panti hekousiazomenǭ	V(a); IV,A,c(i).
hekousion tǭ kuriǭ.	

Preposition + substantive + accusative=construct substantive + substantive + preposition + substantive +	wa'emdexra zentu maŝwā'eta zalf zalalaŝarqa warex
preposition + substantive + za-passive finite verb + la-adjective + substantive =verb + accusative substantive + la-substantive.	wazalala ba'ālāta egzi'abḫēr kwellu qedāsān wazakwellu babafaqādu baṣ'ā la'egzi'abḫēr.

3:6 (3/4)

En hēmerą tę̄ mią	VIII,a(h)
tou mēnos tou hebdomou	
ērksanto anapherein	I,B,1(a)
holokautōseis tǭ kuriǭ	IV,A,c(i)
kai ho oikos tou kuriou	III,A,1,b(i).
ouk ethemeliōthē.	
ama + day-of-month form +	wa'emre'esa šarqa
lašarq + ba-ordinal +	sābe' warex
warex/awrax +	
verb + kama + 3rd plural sub-	axazu yābe'u
junctive + accusative sub-	mašwā'eta
stantive + la-substantive +	la'egzi'abḫēr
substantive, or + construct	wabēta egzi'abḫēr-sa
substantive + substantive +	
___.	itašārarat.

3:7 (12/12)

kai edōken argurion	IV, A,c(i)
tois latomois kai tois	
tektosin kai brōsin kai posin	IV,A,c(i)
kai elaion tois sidōniois	
kai tois turiois	
tou eksenegkai ksula kedrina	I,B,1(b); IV,E,c(n); V(e)
apo tou libanou	IV,F,1(c)
pros thalassan ioppēs	IV,F,1(c); III,A,1,b(j)
dia gnōmēs kurou	IV,F,1(c); III,A,1,b(i)
basileōs persōn	III,A,1,b(j)
ep autois.	III,C(e).

Verb + accusative substantive + *la*-substantive + *la*-substantive + accusative substantive + accusative substantive + accusative substantive + *la*-substantive + *la*-substantive ± *kama* + 3rd plural subjunctive + accusative=construct substantive (less likely: subjunctive-suffix + *la*-construct substantive) + substantive +	*wawahabu warqa laṣarabt walawaqart wamabel'ā-ni wamastē-ni waqebe'ā-ni lasabe'a sēlēmēn wala'ella sārēn kama yāmṣe'u lomu 'eḍawa qadrin*
preposition + substantive + preposition + construct substantive + substantive + preposition + substantive-suffix + *la*-substantive (or construct substantive + substantive) +	*emna libānos xaba bāḥra iyopē wa'emheyya tamayyatu bate'ezzāza qiros*
construct substantive + substantive + preposition + complement.	*neguša fars lā'elēhomu.*

3:8 (3/10)

Kai en tō etei	VIII,a(f)
tō deuterō	
tou elthein autōn	
eis ton oikon	
kuriou tou theou	III,A,1,b(i)
ton en hierousalēm,	III,C(e)
en tō mēni tō deuterō	VIII,a(d)
ērksato zorobabel	formula?
ho tou salathiēl	
kai iēsous	formula?
ho tou iōsedek	
kai hoi kataloipoi	
tōn adelphōn autōn	III,A,1,b(i); III,A,1a(f)
en oikō kuriou.	III,C(e); III,A,1,b(i).

ba-ordinal 'am/'amat + ___ + substantive-suffix + la-substantive, or + construct substantive + substantive, + preposition + substantive +	wabakel'ētu 'āmat emza bashu iyarusālēm westa bēta egzi'abhēr
ba-ordinal + warex/awrax + ___ + substantive-suffix + la-substantive-suffix,	bakāle' warex axaza zarubābēl walda salātyāl wa'iyoses walda iyosēdēq
or + construct substantive + substantive-suffix, + preposition + substantive-suffix + la-substantive, or + construct substantive + substantive.	wa'ella-ni tarfu axāwihomu.

3:9 (8/12)

Kai estē iēsous kai	
hoi huioi autou	III,A,1,a(f)
kai hoi adelphoi autou	III,A,1,a(f)
Kedmiēl kai hoi huioi autou	III,A,1,a(f)
huioi iouda homothumadon	III,A,1,b(i)
tou epinikan	I,B,1(a)
epi tous poiountas ta erga	IV,F,1(c); IV,E,c(n)
en oikō tou theou.	IV,F,1(c); III,A,1,b(i)
huioi ēnadad,	III,A,1,b(i)
huioi autōn kai adelphoi autōn	III,A,1,a(f).
hoi leuitai.	

___ + substantive-suffix +	waqoma iyosēs wadaqiqu
substantive-suffix + ___ +	wa'axāwihu-ni
substantive-suffix + construct	qadāmyāl wadaqiqu
substantive + substantive,	wadaqiqa yehudā-ni
or + substantive-suffix + la-	
substantive, + ___ ± kama +	lā'ela gebr ella yegaberu
subjunctive + preposition +	
substantive ≡ verb + accusative	
substantive (less likely:≡ verb-	
suffix + la-substantive) + pre-	
position + substantive-	bēta egzi'abḥēr
suffix + la-substantive, or	
+ construct substantive +	
substantive. Construct	wadaqiqa inḥad-ni
substantive + substantive, or	
substantive-suffix + la-	
substantive, + substantive-	wadaqiqomu-ni
suffix + substantive-suffix	wa'axāwihomu-ni
___ .	lēwāwiyān.

3:10 (11/12)

kai ethemeliōsan	
hoi oikodomountes	
tou oikodomēsai	I,B,1(a)
ton oikon kuriou	IV,E,c(n); III,A,1,b(i)
kai estēsan hoi hiereis	II,A,2(a)
estolismenoi	
en salpigksi	IV,F,1(c)
kai hoi leuitai	
huioi asaph	III,A,1,b(i)
en kumbalois	IV,F,1(c)
tou ainein ton kurion	I,B,1(a); IV,E,c(m)
epi kheiras dauid	IV,F,1(c); III,A,1,b(i)
basileōs israēl.	III,A,1,b(j).

Verb + ___ +	wašāraru
kama + subjunctive + accusa-	kama yeḥneṣu
tive ≡ construct substantive +	bēta egzi'abḥēr
substantive, or + subjunctive-	
suffix + la-construct substan-	
tive + substantive, or +	
subjunctive-suffix + la-	
substantive-suffix + la-	
substantive, or + subjunctive	
+ accusative substantive-	
suffix + la-substantive, +	
___ + substantive +	wakāhnāt-ni qomu
adjective	lebusānihomu
+ preposition + substantive +	mesla agrent
___ + construct substantive +	walēwāwiyān-sa daqiqa asāf
substantive, or + substantive-	
suffix + la-substantive, +	
preposition + substantive ±	baṣanṣel
kama + subjunctive-suffix +	yesēbeḥewwo
la-substantive (less likely:	la'egzi'abḥēr
+ subjunctive +	
accusative substantive) +	
preposition + substantive-	
suffix + la-substantive, or +	
construct substantive +	batemherta dāwit
substantive, + construct	negušа esrā'ēl
substantive + substantive.	

3:11 (12/15)

Kai apekrithēsan	
en ainǭ kai anthologēsei	IV,B,c(j); IV,F,l(c)
tǭ kuriǭ	
hoti agathon	I,C,2(a); V(a)
hoti eis ton aiōna	I,C,2(a); III,C(e)
to eleos autou	III,A,l,a(f)
epi ton israēl	III,C(e)
kai pas ho laos	V(a)
elalaksan phōnę̄ megalę̄	IV,D; V(a)
en tǭ ainein tǭ kuriǭ	I,B,6(b); IV,B,c(j)
epi tę̄ themeliōsei	IV,F,l(c)
tou oikou kuriou.	III,A,l,b(j); III,A,l,b(i).

Verb-suffix + preposition	wa'awše'u wasabbeḫewwo
+ substantive + substantive	la'egzi'abḫēr wa'akwatewwo
+ la-substantive +	enza yebelu
esma + adjective +	esma xēr we'etu
esma + preposition + substan-	la'ālam
tive + substantive-suffix +	meḫratu
preposition + substantive +	lā'ela esrā'ēl
adjective + substantive +	wayebēlu kwellomu ḫezb
verb + ba-substantive +	baqāl 'abiy
adjective + conjunction +	wayesēbeḫewwo
imperfect-suffix + la-substan-	la-egzi'abḫēr
tive + preposition + construct	soba yešāreru
substantive + construct substan-	
tive + substantive, or +	bēta egzi'abḫēr.
construct substantive + sub-	
stantive-suffix + la-substan-	
tive.	

3:12 (10/16)

Kai polloi	III,C(e)
apo tōn hiereōn	
kai tōn leuitōn	
kai arkhontes tōn patriōn	III,A,1,b(i)
hoi presbuteroi	
hoi eidon ton oikon ton prōton	II,C,1(a); IV,E,c(n); V(a)
en themeliōsei autou	III,C(e);III,A,1,a(f)
kai touton ton oikon	IV,E,c(n); V(a)
ophthalmois autōn	IV,D; III,A,1,a(f)
eklaion phōnē̜ megalē̜.	IV,D; V(a)
Kai polloi en alalagmō̜	III,C(e)
met euphrosunēs	III,C(e)
tou hupsōsai phōnēn.	III,C(a); IV,E,c(n).

Substantive + preposition +	wabezuxān emwesta
substantive + substantive +	kāhnāt walēwāwiyān
construct substantive +	wamalā'ekta abāwihomu
substantive, or + substantive-	
suffix + la-substantive, +	
substantive ± za-verb (less	waliqāwent-ni ella yā'amerewwā
likely: + za-verb-suffix) +	
accusative (less likely: +	lawe'etu bēt
la-substantive) + adjective	zatekāt
+ preposition + substantive-	soba šārarewwo
suffix + accusative (less	
likely: + la-substantive) +	
adjective + ba-substantive +	ware'yewwo lawe'etu bēt
verb + ba-substantive +	ba'aynomu yebakeyu ba'abiy qāl
adjective + substantive	wabezuxān bayebābē
+ preposition + substantive	
+ preposition + substantive	
+ kama + subjunctive +	yeṣareḥu enza yānabebu.
accusative substantive (less	
likely: + subjunctive-suffix +	
la-substantive).	

3:13 (8/10)

Kai ouk ēn ho laos	
epiginōskōn tēn phōnēn	I,A,2,a(c); IV,E,c(n)
semasias tēs euphrosunēs	III,A,1,b(j); III,A,1,b(j)
apo tēs phōnēs	IV,F,1(c)
tou klauthmou tou laou	III,A,1,b(j); III,A,1,b(j)
hoti ho laos	I,C,2(a)
ekraugasen phōnē megalē̜	IV,D; V(a)
kai hē̜ phonē̜ ēkoueto.	

Verb + ___ + accusative ≡ construct substantive (less likely: verb-suffix + ___ + *la*-construct substantive) + construct substantive + substantive + preposition + construct substantive + construct substantive + substantive +	*wa'albo emwesta ḥezb ella yā'ameru qāla* *yebābē feshā* *emna ṣeraḥa* b*ekāyomu*
esma + ___ + verb + *ba*-substantive + adjective + ___.	*esma yeṣareḥu ḥezb baqāl ‘abiy wayessamā‘.*

IV Baruch 1:1 (12.5/16)

wakona	
soba ḏēwawomu	I,3; IV,20
ladaqiqa esrā'ēl	III,5
neguša kalādēwon	III,5
nababo egzi'abḥēr la'ēremyās	IV,25; IV,22 or formula
wayebēlo	
ēremyās xeruyeya	III,3
tanše' waḏā' emzāti hagar	I,1; IV,15; V,1
anta wabārok	
esma halloku amāsenā	I,12; IV,22
embezexa xati'atomu	IV,15; III,5; III,3
la'ella yenaberu westētā.	II,1.

Verb + conjunction + verb +	Egeneto, hēnika ēkhmalōteu-
accusative substantive +	thēsan hoi huioi Israēl
genitive substantive + sub-	apo tou basileōs
stantive + genitive substan-	tōn Khaldaiōn
tive + verb + eis or pros +	elalēsen ho theos pros
substantive + verb + dative	Hieremian
pronoun + ___ + substantive	Hieremia, ho eklektos mou,
+ genitive pronoun + verb +	anasta,
aorist participle +	ekselthe
preposition + substantive +	ek tēs poleōs tautēs
adjective + ___ +	su kai Baroukh:
causal clause= ___ + verb	epeidē apolō
+ accusative pronoun +	autēn
preposition + substantive +	dia to plēthos
genitive substantive + gen-	tōn hamartiōn
itive pronoun + participle +	tōn katoikountōn
preposition + substantive.	en autē.

1:2 (8/9)

esma Šaloteka-ni	VII; III,3
kama ʻamd ṣenuʻ	III,11; V,1
bamā'ekala hagar	III,11; III,5
wakama qeṣr za'admās ʻawdā.	III,11; III,2; III,11.

Substantive + genitive pronoun + *gar* + preposition + substantive + adjective + preposition + substantive + genitive substantive +	*Hai gar proseukhai humōn hōs stulos hedraios estin en mesọ̄ autēs*
preposition + substantive + adjective + preposition + substantive.	*kai hōs teikhos adamantinon perikukloun autēn.*

1:3 (2.5/3)

waye'ezēni	
tanše'u waḫoru waḍā'u	I,1
za'enbala yemṣā' xayla	
kalādēwon waye'udā lahagar	III,5; IV,20.

Aorist predicative participle + aorist predicative partici- ple or finite verb + finite	*Nun anastantes ekselthate*
verb + ___ + substantive + genitive substantive + verb + accusative substantive.	*pro tou tēn dunamin tōn Khaldaiōn kuklosai autēn.*

1:4 (8/9)

wanababa ēremyās	I,6
enza yebel	
āstabaqwe'aka	IV,22
egzi'eya	III,3
azzazo lagabreka	IV,20; III,3
kama yetnāgar qedmēka	I,8; IV,15
wayebēlo egzi'abḫēr	IV,22 or 24
nebab xeruyeya ēremyās.	III,3

Verb + present predicative participle + ___ + verb + accusative pronoun + substantive + genitive pronoun + verb (epitassein?) + dative substantive + substantive + genitive pronoun ± hōste + infinitive + preposition + substantive + verb + dative pronoun, or + pros + substantive, + ___ + substantive + genitive pronoun + ___.	Kai apekrithē Hieremias legōn: parakalō se, Kurie, epitrepson moi tǭ doulǭ sou lalēsai enōpion sou. eipen de autǭ ho kurios: Lalei, ho eklektos mou Hieremias.

1:5 (7.5/13)

wanababa ēremyās	I,1
wayebē egxi'o	
zakwello te'exez	II,1; IV,21
temēṭu-nu zāta hagara xerita	IV,21; V,1; V,1
westa edēhomu lakalādēwon	IV,15; III,6
kama yezzaxar neguš	I,8
mesla ḫezabihu	IV,15;III,3
wayebal	
taxayyalku we'eta hagara	
za'amlāk.	IV,21; V,1; III,2.

Verb + ___ + aorist predicative participle + substantive + hos + finite verb + verb + accusative substantive + adjective + adjective + preposition + substantive + genitive substantive + adverbial clause of purpose=subjunctive + ___ + preposition + substantive + genitive pronoun + verb + verb + accusative substantive + article with demonstrative force + genitive substantive.	Kai elalēsen Hieremias legōn: kurie pantokratōr, paradidōs tēn polin tēn eklektēn eis kheiras tōn Khaldaiōn, hina kaukhēsetai ho basileus meta tou plēthous tou laou autou, kai eipē̦ hoti, iskhusa epi tēn hieran polin tou theou?

1:6 (3/4)

ḫāsa egzi'o	
ema-sa faqādeka	I,14
we'etu ba'edēka	IV, 36 or IV,15; III,3
tamāsenā.	IV,22
___ +	Mē, kurie mou:
adverbial condition clause +	all'ei thelēma sou estin,
dative substantive or preposi-	ek tōn kheirōn sou
tion + substantive + verb +	aphanisthētō.
accusative pronoun.	

1:7 (7/9)

wayebēlo egzi' la'ēremyās	IV,20
esma xeruyeya anta	I,12; III,3
tanše' wadā'u	I,1
anta wabārok	
esma halloku amāsenā	I,12; IV,22
baxati'atomu	IV,15; III,6
la'ella yenaberu westēta.	II,1
Verb + ___ +	Kai eipe Kurios
dative substantive +	tǭ Hieremią:
causative clause=substantive	Epeidē su eklektos
+ genitive pronoun + ___ +	mou ei,
aorist predicative participle	anasta kai ekselthe ek tēs
+ verb + ___ + causative	poleōs tautēs, su kai Ba-
clause= ___ + verb +	roukh: epeidē apolō
accusative pronoun + preposi-	autēn
tion + substantive + genitive	dia to plethōs tōn hamartiōn
pronoun + present participle	tōn katoikountōn en autē.
+ preposition + substantive.	

1:8 (4/4)

wa'ineguš wa'ixayla zi'ahu	
iyekel bawi'a westa hagar	I,19; IV, 15
la'ema ana iqadamku	I,14
wa'iyārxawku anāqeṣihā.	IV,21

___ + verb of conation + infinitive + preposition + substantive + conditional clause= verb + verb + accusative substantive + genitive substantive.	Oute gar ho basileus, oute hē dunamis autou, dunēsetai eiselthein eis autēn, ei mē egō prōtos anoiksō tas pulas autēs.

1:9 (4/4)

tanše' ye'ezēni waḫor	I,1; IV,15
xaba bārok	
wazēnewo zanta nagara.	IV,10; V,1

Aorist predicative participle + verb + preposition + substantive + verb + dative substantive + accusative substantive + adjective.	Anastēthi oun, kai apelthe pros Baroukh, kai apaggeilon autǭ ta hrēmata tauta.

1:10 (8/11)

watanši'akemu	I,2
soba kona sedestu sa'āt zalē-	I,3; V,1; III,2
lit ne'u westa qesra hagar	IV,15; III,5
wa'ana ār'eyakemu	IV,22
wala'ema ana iqadamku amāseno-	I,14; IV,20
ta lahagar iyekelu bawi'ota.	I,19; IV,22.

Aorist participle + verb + conjunction + verb + adjective + substantive + adjective +	Kai anastantes hektēn hōran tēs nuktos, elthete
preposition + substantive + genitive substantive + ___ +	epi ta teikhē tēs poleōs
verb + verb + dative pronoun +	kai deiksō humin
conditional clause= ___ +	hoti ean mē egō
___ + verb + accusative substantive +	apanisō tēn polin,
verb of conation +	ou dunēsetai
infinitive + accusative substantive.	eiselthein eis autēn.

1:11 (2/2)

wazanta behilo egzi'	I,2
xalafa emxaba Ēremyās.	IV,15

Aorist predicative participle +	Tauta eipōn ho kurios,
___ + verb + preposition +	apēlthen apo
substantive.	tou Hieremiou.

The efficiency of the charts of our Chapter Two in predicting the Ethiopic syntax of III ‘ezra 3 was 99.5/135 or 74%. The efficiency of the charts of our Chapter Four in predicting the Greek syntax of IV Baruch 1 was 66.5/84 or 78%. Assuming that these results would have been approximately the same for any prose work from the biblical period, we should conclude that the validity of our analysis of Esther as a starting point in the syntactic analysis of that corpus is established.

Interestingly, the improvements suggested by missed predictions in Esdras and Baruch are more often additions than they are corrections.

Thus in 1 Esdras:

hōs anēr heis (3:1) is regarded as a prepositional phrase for purposes of prediction, pointing up the fact that the analysis has no way to handle a relative clause or an adverbial clause without a verb. Cf. also IV Baruch 1:7 and 1:10.

In 3:2 and 3:3, formulae occur which were not built into the charts of Chapter Two. As noted above, the prediction of formulae is not, strictly speaking, a part of syntactic analysis. However, it might be useful to devise a way to remand formulaic material in advance: perhaps an anterior check "Is there a formula in this verse?" conducted against a list of formulae. Only if the answer were negative would the rest of the syntactic analysis come into play.

In 3:8, 3:9, and 3:10, the infinitive occurs with a preceding genitive article. This construction is not handled in our analysis. For purposes of prediction, we regarded it in these verses simply as an infinitive. However, the addition of the article obviously changes its syntactic function; e.g., tou elthein autōn (3:8) with following subjective genitive, which would not be possible without the article.

In 3:6, finally, the translation of ērksanto anapherein by axazu yābe'u -- scil., by verb + subjunctive -- suggests that our limitation of this usage to cases where the main verb is a "verb of intent" should be modified. Cf. also IV Baruch 1:10.

Similarly in IV Baruch 1, the improvements suggested are on the whole additions:

In 1:1 and 1:7, the Ethiopic construction _hallawa_ + imperfect occurs. No provision was made for it in the charts of Chapter Four since it does not occur in Esther.

In 1:3, _za'enbala_ occurs with the subjunctive, a construction not encountered in Esther and not included in the analysis.

In 1:5, _zakwello te'exez_ can be seen in retrospect as the epithet (formula) _pantokratōr_. Also in 1:5, the use of _elalēsen legōn_ and _eipe hoti_, suggest refinements in the understanding of speech formulae.

Only 1:8, _wa'iyārxawku anāgesihā_, could necessitate any major revision in the analysis as based on Esther 1-8.

As the discussion following Chapters Three, Four and Five suggests, the preparation of a "syntacticon" is cumulative. Every missed prediction is the opportunity for an adjustment in the apparatus of prediction, and each new translation as it is considered affords several such opportunities: omitted constructions are added, misunderstood constructions are reconsidered, syntactic operations treated together are factored out into ordered checks, etc.

Having noted this condition of growth, however, we may bring the present discussion to a close; for nothing would be gained in principle by running further translations through the "syntacticon," and only a little each time would be gained in practice. The mechanical prediction of translation syntax and the recovery from translation of original syntax would seem on the basis of our study to be possible. The mechanization itself would seem to require more, practically, than a doctoral thesis could hope to include.

NOTES

INTRODUCTION

[1]As will be seen in our Chapter Two, the process of reference requires a human operant, but the operant does not operate as a translator. He may be questioned about the form or even about the content of a text; e.g. (p. 89), "Does Y express purpose?" However, he is only questioned about the text in its original language. He is never asked, "How is a purpose clause translated?" It is this question which is answered automatically, by the "syntacticon." The operant programs the "syntacticon" with information which is available either from the text or from lexica before the choice of a translation construction is made. The "syntacticon" makes the choice.

It is important to note that the information supplied by the human operant may not be syntactically relevant in the original language. "Is Y a person?" (p. 100) is syntactically irrelevant in Greek. The answer to the question, though lexically available in Greek, makes a syntactic difference only in Ethiopic. The program of questions on p. 100 thus represents a union of linguistic categories from Greek and Ethiopic and to this extent reflects the syntax of a meta-language: not, certainly, the syntax of an absolute meta-language fixing the inevitable structure of all possible languages but a relative meta-language uniting the structure of two actual languages.

Two approaches to the problem of translation (and to the nature of language) are in play here; we may call them the vertical and the horizontal. The vertical approach maintains that the unvarying deep structure of all language is recoverable with sufficient intuition from any language and, once recovered, is itself the meta-language. The horizontal approach, our own approach in this study, allows for greater genuine differences among languages and only constructs a meta-language cumulatively, adding new parameters as new languages are considered.

Taking the horizontal approach, we assume that when one learns a new language, he does indeed learn something new; i.e., he does not simply see through a new disguise to something already learned or innately known. When a Greek-speaker learns to regard the personal/nonpersonal quality of an Ethiopic noun as relevant to the choice of an Ethiopic genitive construction, we assume that he learns something new; and the assumption shows through in the fact that our program for this choice simply adds a value for this Ethiopic parameter to the values implicit in the fact that the Greek writer has chosen a genitive. Doing this in no way answers the question whether a single deep structure exists in all language or not. However, on a more practical level, doing it successfully or unsuccessfully may indicate whether translation can be efficiently programmed *a posteriori* or whether an omnivalent meta-language must somehow be constructed *a priori* as the matrix into which an utterance in any language must be translated before it can be translated as an utterance in any other language.

[2]Arthur Rimbaud, *A Season in Hell* and *The Drunken Boat*, trans. Louise Varèse (New York: New Directions Paperbook, 1961), pp. 92f.

[3]Cf. Edward Ullendorf, *Ethiopia and the Bible* (London: British Academy, 1968), pp. 36-62.

[4]Francisco Maria Estève Pereira (ed.), *Le livre d'Esther* (*Patrologia Orientalis*, vol. IX, fasc. 1; Paris: Firmon-Didot, 1913), p. 12.

CHAPTER ONE

[1]Included in this section are occurrences of Greek verb X + subject substantive + predicative participle Y; e.g., *badisas Mardokhaios epoiēsen* --> *ḥora mardokēwos wagabra*. In these, it is true, the participle draws its gender and number specification from the subject substantive as well as from the verb. However, the tense of the predicative participle must be understood in relationship to the tense of the Greek predicate; and while the predictability of gender and number in the listed translation constructions may be so complete as to require no further study, the translation predicability of the various tense patterns is still to be established. For this reason we treat a construction that could conceivably be treated under verb-to-substantive subordination in our section on verb-to-verb subordination.

For the same reason, Greek verb X + object substantive + predicative participle Y; e.g., *hupedeiksen tǭ Aman Mardokhaion tois tou basileōs logois antitassomenon* --> *'nagarewwo lahāma kama ya'abi mardokēwos te'ezzāza neguš* (3:4), is treated as verb-to-verb subordination.

[2]The translation of, e.g., *ho de Mardokhaios hupedeiksen*...*tēn epaggelian, hēn epēggeilato Aman tǭ basilei*

--> wanagaro mardokēwos...zakama yebēlo hāmā lanegus (4:7), is "Mordecai showed what sort of promise Aman had made to the king."

[3]E.g., ouden ēthetēsen hōn eneteilato ho eunoukhos (2:15): "He refused nothing," i.e., he did everything; Ethiopic gabrat kwello zakama azzaza zeku xeṣw.

[4]Lexically, though not syntactically, the verse is a mistake. The translator has appently confused diesparmenon, "scattered," from diaspeiro, "to scatter," with diestrammenon, "perverse," from diastrepho, "to twist."

[5]But cf. above, vs. B:2. The use emxaba here corresponds to the use of min to express the agent in biblical Hebrew.

[6]The adjective negušāwi is attested in Ethiopic. However, the language is sparing in the use of adjectives. An English translator who only translated by an adjective where Ethiopic had one would translate perhaps correctly but certainly in an odd style.

[7]The noun neguš is a convenient one to use in comparisons of this sort, since it occurs frequently. However, neguš does introduce another, complicating factor; namely, the fact that honorifics tend to be artificially impersonal. In a recent letter from the general of the Jesuits, I read "It pleased His Holiness to express his love for the Society." Here, even apart from the use of the phrase, "His Holiness," the predicate has been shifted into an artificial impersonal form.

[8]Cf. Chr. Fr. August Dillmann, Lexicon linguae aethiopicae, (New York: Frederick Ungar, 1955 reprint) col. 191 ff.

[9]The citations on p. 50 in Schneider, L'Expression, etc., are to J. Perruchon, Le Livre des mystères du ciel et de la terre, texte et traduction (Patrologia Orientalis, t. I., fasc. 1, 1947, nouveau tirage), p. 9 and p. 20.

[10]Schneider's citation is to Sylvain Grebaut, Le Synaxaire éthiopien IV, mois de Taḫšaš, fin (Patrologia Orientalis, t. XXVI, fasc. 1, 1945, p. 11.

[11]Schneider's citations are to Deborah Lifschitz, Textes éthiopiens magico-réligieux, Le Rempart de la Croix, Abb. 134, feuillet 129 r, p. 154, and to Sylvain Grebaut, Le Synaxaire (cf. note 10 above).

[12]Regarding the case determination of the suffix, cf. Chr. Fr. August Dillmann, Grammatik der aethiopischen Sprache (Graz, Austria: Akademische Druck- u. Verlagsanstalt, 1959; "Unveraenderter Abdruck der zweiten verbesserten und vermehrten Auflage, erschienen 1899 im Verlag von Hermann Tauchnitz in

Leipzig"), pp. 306-307. Since the suffix "...oft das ausdrueckt, was man im Deutschen durch *in Beziehung auf* bezeichnet, so wird natuerlich im Aethiopischen das Pron. suff. nicht nur fuer den Accusativ, sondern auch fuer den Dativ des persoenlichen Pronomens gebraucht..." However, he regards the suffix as basically an accusative, drawing attention to the similarity of the *-a-* linking the suffixes to the verb and the *-a* of the accusative noun. This *-a-* is lost in the subjunctive but only "weil ihm ueberhaupt die kurze straffe Aussprache eigentuemlich ist."

Whatever the suffix may be from the diachronic point of view, from the synchronic point of view it can only be regarded as a generalized oblique case, formally marked only for gender and number, and specified by the context as, variously, the equivalent of *la*-substantive, substantive-*a*, etc.

[13]The Ethiopic verb can take two suffixes but never two of the same person; cf. Dillmann, *Grammatik*, p. 311.

[14]Cf. Eduard Schwyzer, *Griechische Grammatik*, zweite Abteilung, erster Teil, zweiter Band von *Handbuch der Altertumswissenschaft*, herausgegeben von Walter Otto (Muenchen: Beck'sche Verlagsbuchhandlung, 1950), pp. 70 ff., "Akk. des Objekts (im weiteren Sinn)," and pp.140 ff., "Dativ der Beteiligung"; esp. p. 71: "Verba, zu denen einer der drei genannten Akkusative [des affizierten Objekts, des effizierten Objekts, des Ergebnisses] als ihre gewohnheitsmaessige oder noetige Ergaenzung tritt, heissen transitiv. Ausser dem Akkusativ gibt es fuer transitive Verba kein formelles kennzeichen...."; and esp. p. 141: "Der Dativ der Beteiligung steht einerseits in engerer, mehr oder weniger fester und notwendiger Verbindung mit Verben und zugehoerigen Nomina, anderseits in loserer, freierer Fuegung neben solchen; aber auch die Verba der ersten Gruppe werden oft absolut gebraucht."

[15]Martin Heidegger, *Existence and Being*, section "What is Metaphysics?" translated by R. F. C. Hull and Alan Crick (Chicago: Gateway Edition, Henry Regnery Company, 1949), p. 326.

[16]"...originally common..."; *original* here obviously means simply pre-Greek. Synchronically, Ethiopic encounters Greek at a point in its development where the analytic and synthetic complements to the verb distribute along a parameter of animation. Diachronically, this distribution may be far from original; and it may be well to consider at least briefly the sequence of developments that may have led up to it.

The complete confusion of dative and accusative in Ethiopic is an anomaly within Semitic. Nowhere else is the objective suffix so freely used in a dative sense, and nowhere else is the preposition *la*- so commonly used in expressing the accusative. The usages may not be unknown elsewhere. Cf. in Hebrew, Ecclesiastes 2:21: *kî yēš 'ādām še'amālô behokmāh ubeda'at* ubekišrôn ule'ādām šelō' 'āmal bo yittenennu ḥelqo. However, their ubiquitous use in Ethiopic is unique. As a possible explanation of how this confusion came about, we propose the following:

1. After the loss of the Proto-semitic case ending, a noun that was pre-posed and so in deviation from the verb-subject-object prose pattern would have been ambiguous: it could be either subject or object. According to Enno Littmann, such pre-posing was common even in the earliest recorded stage of the language. He writes apropos the syntax of the Axumite inscriptions (Deutsche Aksumexpedition, Band IV (Berlin: Reimer, 1913), p. 81): "Von syntaktischen Eigentuemlichkeiten faellt besonders die Voranstellung des Objekts auf, die ja freilich auch hin und wieder in anderen semitischen Sprachen belegt ist..., die aber hier doch sehr an die spaeter im Semitisch-Abessinischen durch das Hamitische hervorgerufene Wortfolge erinnert."

By way of resolving this ambiguity, la- was prefixed to the preposed element, creating a kind of disjunctive form which would have its syntactic function specified by the presence or absence of an objective suffix on the verb and/or by the addition of a personal pronoun. Subject- as well as object-forms were pre-posed after la-; cf. a surviving example at Esther 9:16: wala'ella tarfu ayhud...tagābu'u emuntu-hi babaynātihomu --> "And as for the rest of the Jews, they assembled by themselves." The objective suffix, already used resumptively in relative clauses where, of course, one element is always pre-posed, would have been readily available for resumptive use in main clauses.

At this stage, since la- + object would not be used unless it was pre-posed, the suffix would not be anticipatory and redundant but resumptive and, at times certainly, necessary. That is, at this stage only two direct object patterns existed: la-substantive + verb-suffix and verb + accusative substantive: labe'esi rakabkewwo or rakabku be'esē.

2. In a second stage, la- + object substantive would begin to be used after the verb as well as before it. At this point, the suffix would not be the syntactic definition of the substantive. Rather the substantive would be the appositive definition of the suffix. It was this shift that led to the introduction of the animation parameter, for la- + substantive was appositive after the substantive suffix, but the suffix on the substantive -- by contrast with the suffix on the verb -- was always personal. Among the Axumite inscriptions, only Inscription 13, ll. 7-8, contains even a possible occurrence of the suffix to the substantive used in a non-personal sense. The sentence is wamada (= wamas'a?) aksum-hā wa'amāsana šeno, which would be translated, "He came to Aksum and destroyed its beauty." However, Littmann indicates that this translation is doubtful (Deutsche Aksum-expedition, Band IV, p. 45). If the

translation is correct, it may indicate that the group of animate nouns is formally constituted of all those that have or could have a proper name; thus, not only gods, men, and animals but also cities (cf. below, Chapter Five, IV Baruch 1:8) and quasi-names such as "earth," "sea," etc. Interestingly, this is a class of words which retains gender when the rest of the language loses it. For further evidence for the existence of an animation-parameter, cf. above pp. 112 ff. In step 4, we will have more to say about how this parameter became current in the verb.

3. At the earliest stage of the language, the dative object was expressed by la- + substantive. However, because of the frequent occurrence of verbs of the class to say and to give with unmarked direct objects -- scil., with clause objects, a re-interpretation occurred in which the dative object after la- was understood to be a direct object.

This re-interpretation had at least two consequences within the class of verbs to say and to give. First, false passive transformations like the English I gave him book --> he was given the book became possible: tamattawa = he received rather than he was given, tanāgara = he spoke rather than he was spoken. Second, the dative object re-interpreted as an accusative could be suffixed to the verb: yebēl lo --> yebelo, yenager lo --> yenagero, yemētu lo --> yemētewwo, etc.

Outside the class of verbs to say and to give, the dative object was more or less likely to be suffixed as it was felt, lexically, to be more or less like the class of verbs to say and to give. A spectrum was created with, at one end, the class of verbs to say and to give, which from an early stage always suffixed the dative object, and, at the other end, the class of verbs indicated on p. 47, which even in the late stages never suffix the dative object. As a rule, the latter seem to be verbs after which the dative means for rather than to.

4. As the distribution of accusative and dative began to blur, i.e., as la- began to express either dative or accusative and the suffix either accusative or dative, a new distribution was suggested by analogy with the noun. The suffix on the noun was neither dative nor accusative but only personal (or at least animate); but since it was explained appositively by la- + substantive, there was enough similarity for the suffix on the verb to be colored by meaning of the suffix on the noun. There was a point of contact, in other words, or there were two points of contact; for the similarity of the construct and the accusative was such that the contrast of (personal) substantive-suffix with (non-personal) construct substantive could be understood to match the contrast of (personal) verb-suffix and (non-personal) verb + accusative.

We must keep in mind that after step 2, verb-suffix + la-substantive and verb + accusative substantive were contrasting usages in search of a contrast. The raison d'être of the analytic form was erased by placing la-substantive after the verb-suffix. It is not surprising then that a contrast was supplied; and when one reflects that even the inflectional endings of the Ethiopic perfect have been replaced by those of the noun, it is not surprising that this contrast was supplied from the noun.

5. In the last stage of the development, the re-interpretation yebēlo is itself re-interpreted as yebē lo. A sentence like yebē lo labe'esi has potential for development in two distinct directions. Attending to the repetition of la-suffix before la-substantive, the speaker could infer an optional pleonastic la-suffix before any la-substantive, whether or not the verb is suffixed; e.g. (Esther C:25) red'ani lita labāḥtāwit; (Esther 6:9) kamaze yekawen lotu labe'esi. Attending to the absence of the suffix on yebē, he could infer that certain verbs do not take a suffix in the dative sense (i.e., at this point a personal suffix) and begin dropping suffixes from verbs he felt to be of this type; cf. the class of verbs discussed above, pp. 46 ff.

What was the effect of the Greek dative/accusative contrast on Ethiopic at this stage in the development of Ethiopic? On p. 44, we stated that this effect was "a partial re-distribution of the two main forms of the complement to the verb along a parameter of independence or emphasis, an imitation of the dative/accusative parameter." The statement is correct as far as it goes; but if the diachronic analysis we have suggested is correct, we may be in a position to understand better why the redistribution was possible.

It was possible because the original dative/accusative contrast was never wiped out entirely. We have spoken of the re-interpretation of the analytic and synthetic complements to the verb on the analogy of the analytic and synthetic complements to the noun. But it is important to note that had the re-interpretation been complete, it would have meant not only an optional -suffix + la- for every personal accusative but also an optional accusative for every non-personal dative. Non-personal dative objects are hardly common, but Esther 3:11 would seem to be an example: ḥezba-ni gebar zakama faqadka "Do what you will to the people." If such occurrences were more common, then the dative/accusative distinction might have been more thoroughly blotted out. They are not common, and so we may say that dative survives as a lack of symmetry in the animation parameter.

The absence of an accusative form with a dative meaning, the survival of some kind of accusative/dative contrast where there were two objects (IV,A), and the influence of Greek as a Vorlage combined to push Ethiopic back toward its original state. That no equilibrium was reached suggests very strongly that Ethiopic became primarily a written rather than a spoken language soon after its first contact with Greek and its first literary use.

[17]Cf. Dillmann, Lexicon, col. 869. Dillmann doess not make the point about word order explicitly, but his examples all confirm it.

[18]The form tazkāri'a is anomalous. Mss. N and P contain the easier reading tazakkari'a.

[19]H. G. Liddell and R. Scott, A Greek-English Lexicon (Oxford: Clarendon, 1940), p. 333 b: "bussinos... II. = porphurous, Hsych."

[20]"Gold crown" and "golden crown" come from two different strata in the development of English modification; i.e., they are not different parts of one original system but rather respectively an innovation and the form which, by rights, the innovation should have replaced. If we attribute different meanings to them, we do so in the thought that where a language has two words for exactly the same thing, usually either one of those words drops out of use, or both remain in use but no longer mean exactly the same thing. There is, in other words, a natural parsimony in language. Our hesitation in suggesting that X-a + Y and X + za-Y have developed a difference in meaning stems from the fact that the parsimony of language is not as relentless as the parsimony of linguistics. If it were, then obviously there would be no linguistics.

[21]Dillmann, Grammatik, p. 466.

[22]The Ethiopic adds the phrase ama 10 wa 3, which is not a translation at all but a gloss, apparently inserted by confusion with 3:12, where Artaxerxes assembles his scribes and passes the decreee of annihilation on the thirteenth of Nisan.

[23]Ethiopic has a set of numerical adjectives distinct from the ordinals and used only for the days of the week and the month. The ordinal type is qātel: šāles, rābeʻ, etc. The diurnal type is qatel: šalus, rabuʻ, etc.

[24]Cf. the word for "year": singular ʻām --> plural ʻāmāt --> doubled plural ʻāmtāt --> back-formation singular ʻāmat, ʻāmat is now much more frequently used than ʻām.

CHAPTER THREE

[1]Francesco Maria Estève Pereira, Le Livre d'Ester, version éthiopienne, Tome IX, Fascicule 1 of Patrologia Orientalis, ed.

R. Graffin and F. Nau (Paris: Firmin-Didot, 1911).

[2]More exactly, the analysis was based on the text given in Pereira corrected at twenty-six points to Q (cf. above, pp. 127-128). The translation patterns established were then checked against the remaining Q variants. Q disagreeed with the analysis at the following points only:

A:11

kai diegertheis Mardokhaios	watanše'a mardokēwos
ho heorakōs to enupnion touto	ware'ya zanta ḥelma
kai ti ho theos bebouleutai poiēsai,	esma egzi'abḥēr faqada yegbar
eikhen auto en tȩ̄ kardia̧;	wa'aqabo westa lebbu;

according to I, A, 1, a and c, this text should be translated watanši'o;

2:1

mnēmoneuōn	yezēker lāti
hoia elalēsen;	bakama tewaš'ato;

according to I, C, 1, b and I, C, 2, a, this text should be translated zakama;

3:13

kai apestalē dia bibliophorōn	wafannawa ḥawāreyāta
eis tēn Artakserksou basileian	westa dawala mangeštu la'artakserksēs
aphanisai to genos tōn Ioudaiōn;	kama yātfe'omu lazamada ayhud;

according to I, B, 1 (p. 15), the singular subjunctive should be a plural: yātfe'ewwomu; the same disagreement with the same word occurs again at 3:9 and B:6.

[3]Q readings chosen because of surface similarity to the LXX were: 3:7, 3:8, 3:13, C;1 (twice), 6:2, 6:6, 6:10 (twice), 6:13, 7:2, 7:3, 8:1, E;10, E:13, E;20, E:24.

Q readings chosen because of grammatical consistency were: 1:19, 2:3, 3:2, 3:8, 4:8, C:7, 6:12, 7:5, E:18.

[4]A:6, 7, 9; 1:4, 5, 18, 19; 2:1, 10; B:2, 4; 3:14; 4:8, 11, 13, 15; C:5, 6, 7, 14, 18, 19; 5:6, 8, 12; 6:3, 5, 13, 18; 7:10; 8:3, 7, 8, 9, 10; E:3, 4, 10, 21, 22.

CHAPTER FIVE

[1]The Greek of I Esdras is taken from Franciscus Vatabli, *Sacra Biblia Hebraice Graece et Latine, cum annotationibus Francisci Vatabli Hebraicae linguae quondam Professoris Regij Lutetiae* (Heidelberg: ex officina Commeliana, M.D.XCIX). The Ethiopic of III ʻezrā is taken from E. Pereira, *Le troisième livre de ʻezra (Esdras et Néhémie canoniques), version ethiopie*[illegible] *[illegible]ologia Orientalis*, tome XIII, Fasc. 5; Paris: Firmin-Didot, 1919). The Greek of Baruch is taken from J. Rendel Harris, *The Rest of the Words of Baruch, a Christian Apocalypse of the Year 136 A.D., the text revised with an introduction* (London: Cambridge University Press, 1889). The Ethiopic of IV Baruch is taken from A. Dillmann, *Chrestomathia Aethiopica, edita et glossario explanata* (Lipsiae: Weigel, 1866).

BIBLIOGRAPHY

Bassano, Francesco da (ed.). Old Testament in Ethiopic. Asmara: Press of the Catholic Mission, imprimatur 1926.

Budge, E.A.W. (ed.). The Book of the Mysteries of the Heavens and the Earth and other Works of Bakhayla Mîkâ'êl (Zôsimâs). London: Oxford University Press, 1935.

Cerulli, Enrico. Storia della letteratura etiopica. Milano: Nuova Accademia Editrice, 1956.

Chaine, M. Grammaire éthiopienne. Beyrouth: imprimerie catholique, 1907. Nouvelle Edition, 1938.

Dillmann, August. Grammatik der Aethiopischen Sprache. Leipzig: T.O. Weigel, 1857.

Dillmann, August. Chrestomathia Aethiopica, edita et glossario explanata ab Augusto Dillmann. Lipsiae: Weigel, 1866.

Dillmann, August. Lexicon Linguae Aethiopicae cum indice Latino. New York: Frederick Ungar, reprint 1955.

Hanbart, Robert (ed.). Esther. Septuaginta, Vetus Testamentum Graecum Auctoritate Academiae Litterarum Gottingensis editum. Goettingen: Vandenhoeck & Ruprecht, 1966.

Harris, J. Rendel. The Rest of the Words of Baruch: A Christian Apocalypse of the Year 136 A.D., the text revised with an introduction. London: Cambridge University Press, 1889.

Jaeger, Ronald (ed.). Essays in Logic, From Aristotle to Russell. Englewood Cliffs, N.J.: Prentice-Hall, Inc., 1963.

Jespersen, Otto. Analytic Syntax. Copenhagen: Levin & Munksgaard, 1937.

Lambdin, Thomas O. Introduction to Classical Ethiopic (Ge'ez). Missoula, Montana: Scholars Press, 1978.

Littmann, Enno. Deutsche Aksum-expedition, Band IV. Berlin: Reimar, 1913.

Littmann, Enno (ed.), with C. Brockelmann, Franz Nikolaus Finck, and Johannes Leipoldt. Geschichte der christlichen Litteraturen des Orients. Leipzig: Amelangs, 1907.

McDaniel, Herman. An Introduction to Decision Logic Tables. New York, London, Sydney: John Wiley & Sons, Inc., 1968.

Pereira, E. (ed.). *Le troisième livre de 'Ezra (Esdras et Néhémie canoniques), version éthiopienne*. *Patrologia Orientalis*, tome XIII, fasc. 5. Paris: Firmin-Didot, 1919.

Pereira, F.M.E. (ed.). *Le Livre d'Esther, version éthiopienne*. *Patrologia Orientalis*, tome IX, fasc. 1. Paris: Firmin-Didot, 1911.

Perruchon, J. *Le livre des mystères du ciel et de la terre*. *Patrologia Orientalis*, tome I, fasc. 1: Paris: Firmin-Didot, 1947.

Schneider, R. *L'Espression des compléments de verbe et de l'adjectif epithète en guèze*. Paris: Librairie Ancienne Honoré Champion, 1959.

Schwyzer, Eduard. *Griechische Grammatik auf der Grundlage von Karl Brugmans Griechischer Grammatik*. Zweiter Band, *Syntax und syntaktische Stilistik*. Vervollstaendigt und herausgegeben von Albert Debrunner. Munich: Beck'sche Verlagsbuchhandlung, 1950.

Ullendorf, Edward. *Ethiopia and the Bible*. The Schweich Lectures of the British Academy, 1967. London: Oxford University Press, 1968.

Vatabli, Franciscus (ed.). *Sacra Biblia Hebraice Graece et Latine, cum annotationibus Francisci Vatabli Hebraicae linguae quondam Professoris Regij Lutetiae*. Heidelberg: ex officina Commeliana, M.D.XCIX.